R. D. Wingert.

THE SOCIAL TEACHING OF JESUS

·The MM Co·

THE SOCIAL TEACHING OF JESUS

An Essay in Christian Sociology

BY

SHAILER MATHEWS, A.M.

PROFESSOR OF NEW TESTAMENT HISTORY AND INTERPRETATION
IN THE UNIVERSITY OF CHICAGO

New York
THE MACMILLAN COMPANY
LONDON: MACMILLAN & CO., Ltd.

1909

451

Norwood Press
J. S. Cushing & Co. — Berwick & Smith
Norwood Mass. U.S.A.

CONTENTS

CHAPTER I

CHAPTER II

CHAPTER III

CHAPTER IV

NOTE

THE following chapters appeared originally as a series of essays in the *American Journal of Sociology*. They have, however, been to a considerable extent rewritten, and are published in their present form with the consent of the editor of that journal.

THE SOCIAL TEACHING OF JESUS

CHAPTER I

INTRODUCTION

THE term Christian Sociology may be used both incorrectly and unfortunately. The names of many sciences are used in two ways: they may indicate the method by which results are obtained, and they may indicate the formulation of such results. Thus history may be a method science or it may be a descriptive science. In the former case it would be absurd to unite with it any word having a moral content. A method of investigation may be ill or well fitted to produce the best results, but ethically it can be neither good nor bad. The same is perhaps even clearer of such objective sciences as chemistry and geology. To speak of a Christian method of sociological investigation is quite as impossible. The process of investigating social forces and results, the discovery of the true nature of society, can no more have an ethical —

still less religious — character than the study of a crystal or a chemical compound.

In the other sense in which the name of a science is used such criticism is less appropriate. The moment an investigator attempts to formulate his results in propositions, that ´moment he injects into them his own predilections. While the method of investigation may be morally neutral, the statement and the application of its results may be largely tinged with ethics. This is less obvious in the case of physical sciences, but admittedly true of the social. Thus in a true sense there may be a Christian view of history, and, so to speak, a Christian science of history. This is even more evident in the case of philosophy. In the sense, therefore, of the formulation and application of results derived by Christian students, a sociology may be said to be Christian.

It is, however, not altogether clear that such a terminology though permissible is advisable. Historically, at any rate, the term is at a disadvantage. The champions of some so-called Christian sociology are dangerously open to criticism similar to that which Voltaire passed upon the Holy Roman Empire — it is neither scientific nor Christian. It certainly is desirable that an end should come to such pious christening of scientific progeny of at best very questionable parentage. With a recognition of its analogy with other scientific terminology, if the term is to be used, we bespeak for it a more definite and positive definition.

This desired definition is to be found in the use of the word Christian in a sense parallel with such adjectives as Hegelian, Aristotelian, Baconian. Just as the philosophies bearing these names are respectively the gifts of Hegel and Aristotle and Bacon, so Christian sociology should mean the *sociology of Christ;* that is, the social philosophy and teachings of the historical person Jesus the Christ. In this positive sense the term is both legitimate and capable of an at least tentatively scientific content.

I

It may be objected that no such philosophy and teachings exist — that Jesus was a teacher of religion and morals and that beyond the realm of these subjects his words are as few as those concerning biology or historical criticism. Such a view, however, is not easily tenable. While it is evident that Jesus has given us no system-atized social teachings, he certainly was no more a

systematic theologian than he was a sociologist.
And, *a priori*, it would be a singular phenome-
non if Christian teaching which has everywhere
effected remarkable social changes should itself be
possessed of no sociological content. It is not
altogether a reply to say that good men must
necessarily produce social improvements. Good
Brahmans in India have not greatly elevated
women, and good Greeks in Athens supported
slavery. Advance in civilization has not been
accomplished by simply producing individuals of
high religious and moral character. Since the
days when the law went forth forbidding the
branding of criminals, Christian impulses have
been quite as much social as individual, and the
yeast of the Kingdom quite as much political as
personal. Is it altogether impossible that He
whose followers have rebuilt empires and founded
new civilizations should have been quite unsus-
picious of the social and political forces that lay
within his words?

It is difficult to appreciate such a possibility for
two reasons. The first lies in the individualistic
philosophy which, since the Reformation, has
largely dominated the theological and exegetical
study of the New Testament. The chief aim of
theology has been the discovery of an explanation

of the "salvation" of each individual believer. A new man and not a new society has been the objective point of most preaching. If sometimes the theologian has been forced into a belief in the solidarity of the race, it has really been that he might have a major premise on which to base his restricted conclusion as to the fate of the individual. Such a point of view was inevitable. No man can escape the *zeitgeist*. But in thus rightly insisting upon the need of saving faith on the part of every man, our religious teachers have to a considerable degree overlooked the essential sociability of human nature, and unconsciously have developed exegetical presumptions that have biassed interpretation. Scriptural teachings have been applied to men as if they were insulated entities, and to society as if it were but an aggregation of easily separated wholes.

The results of such presuppositions are no less unfortunate than inevitable. They have affected not merely the conception of the position of the church in the world, but they have also narrowed Christian truth to a field in which Jesus never meant it to remain, and to which the early Christians did not limit it. Perhaps to-day's thought is swinging to the other extreme ; but at the worst, modern conceptions of man and society are calcu-

lated to offset the unmodified individualism of the
past.   Philosophy, it is true, should never dictate
interpretation, but what conscientious exegete
would dare claim absolute immunity from its influence?   Whether for weal or woe, the underlying
premises of the social sciences that isolation is
abnormality and that society is itself an object of
study, promise some day to prove as revolutionary
in biblical interpretation as was the new conception of the worth of the individual in the sixteenth
century.   The results of the past may thus be
supplemented by those of the present.   The
future of a man is known ; the future of mankind
is now to be discovered.   And this discovery will
in no small way spring from a new appreciation
of the teachings of Jesus.

A second obstacle in the way of formulating the
social teachings of Jesus is the impatient and over-
zealous publication of certain doctrines that are
called Christian, but which are based, not upon
exegesis, but upon a philanthropy largely unre-
strained in both its prejudices and its rhetoric.
Disregarding the mischievous tendency for every
good man to dub as " sociology " his hasty thinking and hopes as to society; disregarding the
refreshing certainty enjoyed by many amateur
though earnest reformers that in the preparation

of millenniums the accumulation of figures and statistics is wholly superfluous ; disregarding the fact
that much so-called sociological teaching is nothing more than relabelled ethics ; granting that
sociologies are as easy to produce as political panaceas, the fact remains that as yet Christian sociology has been too much at the mercy of men who
have mistaken what they think Christ ought to
have taught for what he really did teach. Nothing is easier for the brain fertile in generalities
and for the heart burning with sympathy and indignation than to evolve a system from a sentence
or a term. In this particular Christian sociology
is re-running the career of Christian theology. As
the dogmatic theologian has too often made a system of philosophy masquerade as a theology by
dressing it out with a series of more or less well-
fitting proof-texts, so too often modern prophets
to a degenerate church, in sublime indifference to
the context, time of authorship, and purpose of a
New Testament book, and with an equal neglect
of the personal peculiarity and vocabulary of a
New Testament writer, have set forth as the word
of Christianity views which are but bescriptured
social denunciation and vision. If this be Christian sociology, it is little wonder that the genuine,
albeit less inspired, student of social phenomena

and Christian teaching should view it with suspicion and question the worth of an attempt to
discover any such phantasmagoria in the words
of the Teacher of Nazareth.

II

There is but one way to the apprehension of
the teachings of Jesus, whether religious or social,
and that is the patient study of the gospels
with the aid of all modern critical and exegetical
methods. The only thoroughly safe method is
the inductive gathering of teachings from the
gospel sources, and their subsequent classification into a system. Here, as in all scientific
processes, the aim of the investigator must be
the discovery of what is, not the substantiation of
some notion as to what ought to be. It is even
unsafe, as a first step, to gather only such passages as may serve as the basis of a particular
doctrine. The first question is not *what* sociology
did Jesus teach, but *whether* he taught anything
that may properly be called sociological. Classification must logically, and generally chronologi-
cally, succeed discovery and interpretation. Let
all the materials for a social teaching first be
gathered. Then, whether they be few or many,
let them be shaped into a system.

Such a method is not peculiar to the study of the New Testament. It is that by which one must gain the system of any writer who has himself not arranged his thoughts in a formal order. To such a method the words of Jesus are as the words of Plato. The greatest reverence that may be shown them is to treat them as if they needed no exegetical odds, and are not only intelligible and capable of enduring rigid scrutiny, but the expressions of a mind that was sane if not systematic.

But in such a method the words of Christ have more than an archæological or devotional import. The student of occidental civilization who disregards his teachings is as unscientific as he who in the history of philosophy should neglect Plato and Kant, or in the history of the United States of America should disregard the Constitution. No man's teaching has equalled his in the magnitude of its social results, and there may be messages in his words yet worth hearing. But on the other hand, quotation is not exegesis, and rhetoric is not classification. If Jesus is to figure among sociologists, before he is cited as an authority let him at least be understood. And if he is to be debarred from the class of social teachers, let it first be remembered that much which is put

forth as his is no more from him than the schoolman's gloss was from Aristotle.

III

The sources from which it is possible to draw
the social teachings of Jesus are primarily, though
not exclusively, his own words. At first glance,
therefore, no problem could seem easier than the
process of gaining such teachings. With most
theologians of the past, with many of to-day,
the *ipsissima verba* of the Master are an end of
all discussion. But even if we disregard the possible changes incident to one or more processes
of translation, it is a prime necessity that the
interpreter remember that thought is superior
to word, and that a sentence wrenched from its
context may be quite as misleading as a similarly
detached word. The thought of Jesus is sometimes so genuinely Oriental as to elude any
process of interpretation that is purely verbal.
His style is so concrete, and his similes so perfect,
that there is a constant temptation to forget that
a parable, after all, can enforce only an analogy,
and that the real teaching of its author lies not
in its form but in the analogy. Further than
this, Jesus seldom combined complementary or
mutually modifying thoughts. He was not a

systematic lecturer, but a creator of impulses. He sometimes puts forth a proposition so categorically as to make it appear that it exhausts his teachings upon the subject, and yet under some other circumstances its modification is expressed with equal absoluteness. The two superficially appear contradictory. In reality they are the two hemispheres of the truth. To claim either of them alone as his teaching is to do Jesus injustice. His real teaching can be gained only through their combination. For this reason, so far as a systematized and complete statement is concerned, outside of the magnificent summaries into which Jesus has compressed the essentials of religion and morals, no one can claim to have mastered Christian teaching until he has mastered its entirety. The failure to observe this simple caution lies at the bottom of much of the heresy and sectarianism of the centuries, and of no little crude religious instruction to-day.

It is, therefore, above all necessary to study the words of Jesus not only as detached maxims, but as the scattered parts of a complete system of which they are the outcroppings and in the statement of which they may be harmonized. If this central principle be first discovered, many otherwise hard sayings will be seen to be simply striking forms in which it is applied to special needs.

At this point one naturally meets the question, Are the teachings of Jesus commensurate with the teachings of the entire New Testament? In a certain sense it is perhaps true that Christian doctrine is thus commensurate. Waiving in this discussion the question of the inspiration of the apostolic writers, it is yet reasonable to hold that in the teachings that emanated from the companions of Jesus we have that which must be regarded as expressive of the spirit and purpose of Christ. Nevertheless, it would be contrary not only to the most ordinary processes of historical study but also to the testimony of Christian consciousness if no distinction were made between the social teachings of the gospels and those of the epistles. In the latter we have the application of the former to the needs of the growing Christian societies of the first century. In some cases these applications are clearly adapted only to the peculiar circumstances — the "present distress" — of those early years. At all events, it is very apparent that in the passage from the social teachings of the four gospels to those of the other New Testament writings, we are passing from a constitution to statutory law, from principle to attempted realization of principle, from philosophy to conduct. For this reason, it is better to confine the search for the data of Christian sociology, as it is defined above, to the gospel narrative and its brief continuation in the opening section of the Acts.

Yet even here the circle whence these data are to come must be somewhat further restricted. Wholly apart from the question as to the origin and mutual relations of the four gospels, it is beyond serious question that in their present form the accounts they contain are the work of writers who lived at least a generation after the death of Jesus. The sources of each gospel can be shown to date from the contemporaries of Jesus, and it is possible that at least three of the accounts were brought into their present literary form by these contemporaries themselves. Yet however this may be, the gospels now clearly contain two elements : the teachings of Jesus, and the editorial material added to them by their writers.

This second element is considerable in the Fourth Gospel, but by no means wanting in the synoptics. It is of various sorts, but may be mostly classified as introductions, transpositions, explanations, reflections, prophetic antitypes, and verbal changes. Many of these are self-evident to the careful reader, and most are easily sepa-

rated from the teachings of Jesus by simple processes of criticism. Their value is considerable,
however, for the understanding of Jesus' own
positions, upon which they form a sort of commentary or scholium. In few cases will their
separation affect the force of the passage from
which they are taken, but it is evident that such a
separation might at times be of service in ap-
preciating the teaching of Jesus himself.

One other form of editorial work is, however,
of the utmost value as a source of the social teachings of Jesus — the narrative of his life. In most
cases such narrative is demonstrably from eyewit-
nesses and in its essential elements is beyond
suspicion. From such narrative data may be
drawn of equal importance with those contained
in the words of Jesus. His example and life,
quite as much as his spoken teachings, have
universally been accepted as a basis for Christian
doctrine, but nowhere are they of more importance
than in the sphere of his social teaching. No
student of the life of Jesus would venture to predi-
cate inconsistency between his outward act and his
inward belief. It is impossible to think of him,
simply as an honest man, practising that which
he would forbid his followers. In certain cases,
it is true, he did accommodate himself to circum-

stances and demands that he regarded as peculiar and even unjust, but seldom without specific explanation or comment. Speaking generally, the doings of Jesus, when once viewed in the light of their attending circumstances, quite as much as his words, are materials from which to construct a systematized statement of his social teachings.

There is still another source of such teaching which, though negative, is not to be disregarded — the silence of Jesus on many points upon which the age in which he lived was interested quite as much as is our own. For example, such social evils as slavery, gambling, prostitution, are unassailed in the gospel narrative. So far as many deeper social and political questions are concerned Jesus was also silent. This fact is not only remarkable, it is significant of a distinct element in what we venture to call his social philosophy. Just what this element was does not concern us here. It is enough to call attention to the fact and to suggest that a vocalization of this silence, be it with never so eloquent a philosophy or never so ingenious play upon words and texts, is to make exposition presuppose, if not dangerously resemble, imposition.

IV

If one adopts the conventional division of the study of sociology — descriptive, static, and dynamic — it at once becomes evident that little that can be termed descriptive sociology is to be found within the gospels. Jesus was not a student of society in the technical use of the term. His interest in publicans and sinners was not simply scientific, and his work was not that of the investigator, but of the revealer and inspirer. It is impossible to think of him as laboriously gathering material for a treatise upon social phenomena — a measurer of foreheads and a compiler of statistics. Not only was the age in which he lived innocent of any such scientific processes, but the whole career of Jesus makes it evident that while no man — not even Socrates — ever possessed a keener perception of human nature alike in its strength and weakness, his main effort was the presentation of ideals and the gift of spiritual powers through which they might be attained. For this reason any systematized presentation of his teachings must content itself with a very incomplete and incidental presentation of his views of humanity as it is, and devote itself almost exclusively to his conceptions of what society may become, and the means and process through which its desired consummation may be reached. If it should appear that Jesus occasionally characterized life as he found it, it will also be clear that such characterization was but a part of this effort at portraying an ideal society and the enforcing of effort for its attainment.

c

CHAPTER II

MAN

WHILE from many considerations it would be advisable to begin the examination of Christ's social philosophy with a study of the Kingdom of God, it is at once obvious that logically the doctrine of the individual precedes the doctrine of society. With Jesus, as with all thinkers, the possibilities of the component parts of a social whole must limit the possibilities of that whole. With him, "sociology as a whole rests primarily upon psychology." [1] If in the thought of Jesus man is not a social being, but rather is a repellent whole, his conception of society must be radically different from that of an organism. If, on the other hand, Jesus regards man as living not merely within the insulated limits of his own individuality, but as essentially a social being, reaching normality only in social life; and if it should further appear that Jesus further regards this

[1] Ward, *Psychic Factors of Civilization*, p. 2.

18

social personality of a man as distinctively human
as is the egoistic, then it is evident that normal
humanity may in some way resemble an organic
whole, and its development the growth of an organism. Within the limits of this conception of
what human beings are and can be, will be found
of necessity his conception of what they and
humanity should be. For if it would beget duty,
the ideal must be possible.

I

It is at the outset necessary to set clear limits
to expectation in regard to the character of the
Christian anthropology. Incomplete data do not
warrant complete systems. Even in Plato a phys-
iological psychologist finds little worthy of serious
consideration, and the psychologist proper is often
obliged to content himself with pregnant analogies when he seeks definitions.

Writers upon biblical psychology have for many
years debated as to whether the human life is
trichotomous or dichotomous. In favor of the tri-
chotomist view [1] it is urged that such expressions
as "may your spirit and soul and body be preserved entire," [2] "piercing to the separation of soul

---

[1] See especially Delitzsch, *Biblical Psychology*.
[2] I Thess. 5 : 23.

and spirit," [1] affirm a threefold division of man's nature. And it must be admitted that the settlement of the question is not altogether easy. The difficulty lies quite as much in the variety of expressions as in their indefiniteness. The older Jewish Scriptures were written at such different times and by such a variety of authors that, so far from having a common, to say nothing of a definite psychology, it is impossible to formulate even those persistent presuppositions which might be expected to underlie popular vocabularies.

The same difficulty lies to a considerable degree in some of the writings of the New Testament collection. But here the smaller number of writers, as compared with that of the older literature, makes the diversity of opinion less apparent, and to a considerable degree makes the discovery of definitions less difficult. Yet no one of these authors was a trained student of experimental science. Paul, the best educated of them all, gives little evidence of any training beyond the severely scholastic methods of the professional schools at Jerusalem. It is true he has the schoolman's accuracy in the use of terms, but he suffers also from the schoolman's lack of scien-

[1] Heb. 4 : 12. To these passages might be added several from the Old Testament, as well as Matt. 22 : 37 and parallels.

tific experiment. In a word, he is not a scientist but a moralist.

If this last be true of Paul it is truer of Jesus. He did, indeed, know what was in man, but his was a knowledge like that of Socrates — a practical and accurate intuition of human nature, rather than the accumulated facts of the psychologist. He has left no attempt to reduce to a system the various phenomena which the student is to-day taught to observe in consciousness. To him the soul was neither a specimen nor a laboratory, but the supreme treasure of the man. For this reason it is idle to search in his teachings for a detailed exposition of its powers. Nevertheless, the terms of his thinking were not without definition. It is a contradiction to suppose that one who thought so keenly thought at the same time vaguely. If one makes due allowance for a colloquialism that was inevitable from his method of teaching, it is at once apparent that with Jesus, as with Socrates, words were the representatives of things. For this reason it is, that, although definitions are uncommon, Jesus' terminology is consistent as well as concrete. The rabbis like all scholastic nominalists might haggle over words. Jesus took them as he found them, and used them steadily as the implements of real thought, able to make deep and consistent impressions without attempting formal distinctions.

Perhaps it is because of this consistency that the difficulties mentioned above are far less evident in the gospels than in the epistles. The unity of their teaching is the unity of a dominating personality. Peter and James and Paul and John and the other authors of letters, each had his own more or less consistent psychological terminology, and in their combination these terminologies are sometimes confusing. But in the words of Jesus such confusion is wanting, for the gospel writers do not allow themselves sufficient editorial license to affect the fundamental conceptions of their Master.[1]

It is these fundamental conceptions that one must seek if one would get the logical point of departure for not merely the social but the reli-

[1] It is, of course, here quite unnecessary to go into any complete discussion of biblical psychology — even if there be any such. It may, perhaps, be noted in passing that any method that attempts to set forth scriptural teachings by a mere aggregation of texts is always liable to the uncertainties and suspicions that will be found to attend any unhistorical search after any developing truth. Besides, it is only too easy to erect a merely practical into an absolute distinction. *Cf.* Broadus, *Commentary on the Gospel of Matthew*, p. 366 n. See also Orr, *The Christian View of God in the World*, p. 160 *sq.* and especially Laidlaw, *Bible Doctrine of Man.*

gious teachings of Jesus. It is not impossible that in the search for them modern ideas may be read into ancient words, but none the less is the search to be made. And if it should appear that beneath prayer and analogy, maxim and exhortation, there should lie a common conception of an ideal that is to be found among the possibilities of every member of the race, and of psychical capacities that make this ideal a possibility, it would be nothing more than one would expect of a thinker at once so artistic and profound as Jesus.

II

With Jesus man is essentially body and soul, flesh and spirit — an incarnate soul or life. But the two elements are not of equal worth. As the body is more than clothing, so is the soul more than the body. The body is destructible, but the soul may be saved, although it may also be (morally) destroyed.[1] Jesus does not, like many thinkers, regard the body as necessarily evil. It is simply subordinate. So long as the race is in this æon, the body is necessary. Upon it depend both the perpetuation of the race through marriage,[2] and, also, death.[3]

This view of man was not altogether peculiar

---

[1] Matt. 10:28.   [2] Mark 10:8; 12:25.   [3] John 6:51, 53.

to Jesus. The teaching of the Jewish schools of his time illustrates and, doubtless, to some extent explains his position. According to rabbinical authorities, mankind consisted of body [1] and soul, the former composed of dust, the other descended from God.[2] Further it was held that the soul was preëxistent [3] and was the salt that kept the body from corruption.[4] The gospels nowhere give foundations for the popular notion that the soul is a lower, more physical life-principle, and the spirit a higher, more divine substance. Indeed, it would be quite as reasonable to quote the development of Jewish thought for a precisely opposite view. Still less is there to be found in the words of Jesus the remoter conception of the soul as a sort of connecting link between the body and the spirit.

Just what the relationship is that exists between the soul and the body Jesus does not describe. If the words put into his mouth by Luke, " a spirit hath not flesh and bones as ye see I have," [5] were actually his, he apparently distin-

[1] At first of double sex. The woman was taken from the man. Weber, *Lehren des Talmud*, 203.

[2] Gen. 2 : 7.   [3] Weber, 204.

[4] See in addition the curious teaching in regard to the threefold origin of a man quoted in Hershon, *A Talmudic Miscellany*, p. 67.

[5] Luke 24 : 39

guished between a ghost and a genuine human personality. But these words introduce so many difficulties, both critical and philosophical, that it will hardly be advisable to rest much argument upon them until they have been given a more careful examination than is here desirable.

In general Jesus distinguished between only physical and spiritual phenomena, and his language, though never technical, is yet sufficiently definite to make it certain that he never held to the trichotomy that possibly characterized the cruder psychology of the early Hebrew scriptures. At all events, the one class of phenomena did not spring from the other. That which is born of the flesh is flesh. Only that born of the spirit is spirit.[1]

It would certainly be inadmissible to consider his reply to the lawyer, "Thou shalt love the Lord thy God with all thy heart, and with all thy soul, and with all thy understanding,"[2] as anything more than a Hebrew cumulative emphasis.[3] So far was Jesus from being a trichot-

[1] John 3 : 6.

[2] Matt. 22 : 37. These words are variously reported by the other evangelists. They are a quotation of Deut. 6 : 4 sq., apparently modified by popular Greek psychological expressions.

[3] It is true, however, that there seems at times a shade of difference between ψυχή (life, soul) and πνεῦμα (spirit). Thus in

omist as sometimes to seem to approach a sort of psychological monism, in which the unity of body and soul constitutes a single life.[1] However this may be, the significance of Paul's treatment of the resurrection of Jesus, the type of the race, lies not least in the support it gives to the belief that a man can never become a disembodied spirit. His future immortality is to be clothed in a new, though inexplicable body, or sensuous nature.[2] A belief in a union of the physical and psychical lies also behind the account of the birth of Jesus as it is contained in the infancy sections of Matthew and Luke, and even more clearly in

Matt. 23 : 35, and Luke 6 : 9 ; 12 : 19, the soul is apparently physical life, the sensuous nature, while "spirit" is generally used when the thought is concerned with moral and religious matters, and especially with the soul's divine origin. Yet it is also true that in Matt. 10 : 28 the former of the words overlaps in meaning that of the other, while in Matt. 27 : 50, Luke 8 : 55, the reverse is the case. And these are by no means the only instances. See in addition Wendt, *Fleisch und Geist*, p. 46.

[1] Such is the implication of the destruction of the body in Gehenna (Matt. 5 : 29, 30; 10 : 28). For even if due allowance is made for the figurative language, the reference is clearly to moral suffering. In Matt. 6: 25 the Hebrew parallel arrangement may not impossibly hint at a similar conception. Yet these and similar passages imply nothing as to an identity of the physical and psychical substances.

[2] 1 Cor. 15: 23, 44 ; 2 Cor. 5 : 1–4. Compare the opinion of Rabbi Judah the Holy, "God will reunite soul and body, and judge them both as one together."

the noble conception of the writer of the Introduction to the Fourth Gospel, "the word became flesh and tented among us." [1]   In each of these cases we have a very early formulation of the philosophy of the incarnation, and one that may very well be taken as representative of the teachings of Jesus himself.

It certainly, therefore, is not too much to say that in the thought of Jesus, the individual man is a unity, which is the outcome of the organic combination of two complementary elements, body and soul.   Humanity in its unit is thus a union.

III

One essential characteristic of this physico-psychical being is its capacity to merge its life with that of similar beings — that is, its capacity for social life.   The ideal human life, as Jesus conceives of it, consists in transcending the limits of an egoistic individuality.   By this it is not meant to maintain that Jesus taught a pantheism or a generic humanity that is a sort of scholastic *mélange*.   Sociability does not mean the extinction of individuality.   It means simply that in the conception of Jesus the self is altruistic as well as

[1] John 1 : 14.

selfish, social as well as individualistic.[1] There are attracting and correlating powers of the personality that reach out to others and form, much like chemical atoms, a new substance that is essentially a unity derived through union.   To disregard the promptings and needs of this social part of the personality is to invite an intellectual and moral death whose earliest symptoms are sin and abnormality of all sorts.   Just as the complete life of the individual depends upon the union of the soul and body does the normal life of the personality demand a similar union with other personalities.   The failure of theology to emphasize this fact is the outcome of a psychology that has been so much concerned with the deliverances of a single consciousness as to slight evidences of social psychical forces.

In the time of Jesus men recognized more or less distinctly the need of establishing a social unity if right living was to be attained — even when their knowledge had little effect upon social institutions.   " Man," says Philo,[2] " is a social ani-

---

[1] See Bax, *The Ethics of Socialism.*   Whatever one may hold as to many positions taken in this essay, it is at least worthy of notice that apparently from a purely non-scriptural, and to some extent anti-scriptural position the author has occasionally arrived at conclusions which are but a paraphrase of the teachings of Jesus.

[2] See the article by Montefiore, " Florilegium Philonis " in the

mal by nature. Therefore he must live not only
by himself, but for parents, brothers, wife, children, relatives and friends, for the members of
his deme and of his tribe, for his country, for his
race, for all mankind. Nay, he must live for the
parts of the whole, and also for the entire world,
and much more for the Father and the Creator.
If he is, indeed, possessed of reason, he must be
sociable, he must love the world and God, that
of God he may be beloved."

The corresponding position of Jesus, though
not expressed so minutely, is quite as distinct
and is far more fundamental to his philosophy.
Men's capacity for union renders attainable the
purpose of his teaching and his life. It is deep
in the ideal which he sets before mankind.

IV

Nowhere does this conception of the necessity
of union more predominate than in those teachings that are the most characteristic of the mind
of Jesus and which are the most valuable and
resultful of all times — the ideal relations that
may exist between the human soul and God.

Jewish Quarterly Review, April, 1895. Philo may be taken as a
representative of a school of thought that both preceded and survived Jesus.

This ideal union is expressed continually and
with great variety. The vine with its branches[1]
symbolizes that relation between Jesus and his
followers, which, whatever attitude one may hold
towards current evangelical theology, is universally felt to include the relation of the divine
and human. His followers are through him to
be one, not only with each other, but with God,
and thus constitute one great family.[2] In his
Father's home[3] were, to use his incomparable
figure, many mansions, in which he and they were
to live. And in his invitation so artistically introduced by Matthew, there is proffered to the weary
and the heavy laden a companionship that shall
at once make them yoke-fellows with himself and
friends of the Father.[4]

It is in illustration of this unity of human life
with that of the divine that Jesus repeatedly sets
himself forth in mystical language as the food of
the soul, the bread that came down from heaven.[5]
And if at times his language grows more striking
than our colder western imaginations often vent-

[1] John 15: 1, 2. It is, perhaps, not without significance that
Jesus here speaks of himself as the *true* vine — as if the relationship thus described was not confined alone to that between himself
and men, but that such union was characteristic of men.

[2] John 17: 23. Compare with this, John 13: 20.

[3] John 14: 2, 3.   [4] Matt. 11: 27–30.   [5] John 6: 32, 35.

ure,[1] and indeed becomes a hard saying even to
his disciples, he instantly explains his analogy in
terms that are at once profound and intelligible.
The same is true of the symbolical teaching of the
Eucharist.[2] So great and essential did this relationship appear to the earliest church that the
whole significance of Jesus as a mere ethical
teacher is overtopped by it, and in the writings of
Paul and John it becomes the leading conception
of both the person and the influence of the Christ.
He was the incarnate God — the perfect realization of this capacity for union between the human
and divine, and at the same time the channel
through whom the race itself might be brought
into union with God, that it might enjoy those
blessings promised God's sons. Indeed, it is not
too much to say that Christianity as a system is
but an unfolding of the conception of the Godward
social capacities of mankind. From this point of
view the cardinal doctrines of the incarnation,
faith, atonement, justification, and immortality,
cease to be abstract, and appear rather the formulation of actual religious experience and the description of psychical possibilities and phenomena.[3]

[1] See especially John 6: 51–64.
[2] Matt. 26 : 26–30 and parallels. *Cf.* 1 Cor. 11 : 23-26.
[3] While superficially the current of theological teaching seems to

V

In a very true sense Jesus identifies the powers
of the soul that make union with God an essential
of the normal man, with those that force a normal
man into union with other human beings. If a
man be imperfect who is apart from the divine, so
is he who is apart from his fellows. Wherever
Jesus holds up a picture of a man's ideal, he makes

have drifted away from this point of view — especially under the
influence of the "Nature" philosophy of the last century — it is
nevertheless true that the doctrine of the so-called Vital or Mystical
Union has been characteristic of many if not most of the chief.
theologies.   Thus Augustine (Serm. 144) : "Qui ergo in Christum
credit, credendo in Christum, venit in eum Christus, et quadam-
modo unitur in eum." So, too, Calvin, *Works* (Brunswick ed., 1870),
IX., 30 : "We coalesce with Christ in a sacred unity and the same
flesh breathes life into us." The *Larger Catechism*, Question 66,
expresses the fact more formally : "The Union which the elect have
with Christ is the work of God's grace, whereby they are spiritually
and mystically, yet really and inseparably, joined to Christ as their
head and husband; which is done in their effectual calling."   See
H. B. Smith, *System of Christian Theology*, p. 531 *sq.*, and a notable
essay on the *Mystic Unicn of the Believer with his Saviour*, in
Sanday and Headlam, *Commentary on the Epistle to the Romans.*
Recently the importance in theology, not merely of this religious
union but of social activity as well, has considerably increased.   If
one cares to see how the terminology of a theological past may yet be
found full of the spirit of Jesus and applicable to modern conditions,
he cannot do better than read Hyde, *Social Theology.*   See also Freemantle, *The World as the Subject of Redemption*, and Westcott, *Social
Aspects of Christianity*, and *The Incarnation and Common Life.*

this second element of the twofold extension of personality not only essential but fundamental. The perfect man, if he be true to his nature, must live in fellowship not only with God but with man.[1]

To begin with his conception of the kingdom. If it were allowable to anticipate somewhat the later discussion of this term, it would appear that man is to become righteous — that is, normal — through life in a normal and righteous social order. This new phase of civilization, further, is not a mere aggregation of unrelated individuals, but is a family. The king is a father and the subjects are brothers. It is no insignificant fact that in certain of its aspects, notably its perfection, the life of an isolated individual received little attention from Jesus. Indeed, when the fate of some single person was in question, as for instance " the disciple whom Jesus loved," [2] his words became enigmatic and, for his immediate audience, unintelligible. His mission included the salvation of

---

[1] Primitive, that is pre-Pauline, Christianity recognized this distinctly. Indeed, James makes the true content of religion consist in social service. James 1 : 26, 27.

[2] John 21 : 22. In the case of Simon Peter (Luke 22 : 30) we have an apparent exception to this general attitude and others also occur. But in all of them it is easy to perceive a purely personal interest.

D

individual souls; but salvation with Jesus, so far as his words are witnesses, did not consist in living a detached life. The kingdom can no more be disintegrated into unrelated lives than righteousness can be gained by society *en masse.* In this outer dependence of the individual and society, Jesus clearly recognizes human life as essentially social.

This conclusion is by no means the truism that it may seem. Among religious teachers, at least, social life has not generally been held to be the normal life for the man who seeks an ideal development. Withdrawal from society, monachism, the literal flight from a corrupt world — these have been the characteristics of the great mass of the religions of the past. Modern evangelicism is often guilty of the same mistake in its attempts to distinguish and withdraw from "worldly" influences. But with Jesus the entrance into a transformed society, the kingdom,[1] is the goal and the reward of the individual's endeavor. He is above all to seek such entrance; within it is he to heap up true riches: to miss it is the saddest lot; to gain it is the consummation of happiness.

[1] Matt. 5 : 20; 7 : 21; 18 : 1 *sq.*; 19 : 23; 25 : 34; John 3 : 3 and numerous other sayings. In the same line are those sayings in which the kingdom is the reward to be reached by men of high morality, *e.g.*, the poor in spirit, Matt. 5 : 10, the humble and child-like, Mark 10 : 14, 15.

In sharpest opposition to all this is the Christian conception of the un-ideal, the abnormal, the sinful condition of mankind. In a word this may be described as one of unsocial relationships. The evil man is a dead limb,[1] a lost sheep, a lost coin, a lost son.[2] It is a little remarkable that although the earliest Christian writings have much to say upon the results of such a condition, Jesus is silent as regards universal sinfulness. With him it would appear as if sin were the reverse of sociability, and a sinful race, as distinct from sinful individuals, a contradiction of terms. In failing to follow the fundamental instincts and capacities of his nature, a man becomes at once selfish, unsocial, and sinful. His punishment is the outcome of his abused nature. Destined for companionship with high spiritual beings, he necessarily turns in upon himself, grows less and less capable of opening his nature to him who seeks his love. He loses those powers by which he might become a member of God's family and of the brotherhood of man. Exclusion from the kingdom is his natural punishment — he is not fit to be one of its members.[3] In one case at least,[4] Jesus states this cause explicitly. At the day of judgment the

[1] John 15 : 6.
[2] Luke 15 : 3–32.
[3] Matt. 8 : 12; 21 : 43.
[4] Matt. 25 : 34–46.

ground on which exclusion from the kingdom will be based is a failure to fulfil the social duties of the present age. Hell is thus at once the opposite and the horrible caricature of heaven, for it is not merely an accommodation of his thought to Jewish terminology when Jesus describes the selfish rich man as suffering alone in Gehenna, and the poor man as in the companionship of Abraham.[1] Translated into the language of to-day this parable illustrates a principle that would not be altogether different from this : As long as a kingdom and a brotherhood are the goal of human effort, so long must man be capable of social life, and sociability a characteristic element of a normal man. The degeneration of the social nature that arises from the neglect of social duties, unfits a man for, or participation in, the enjoyments of the ideal life. Selfishness — that is, an over-developed individualism — must according to the laws of nature result in abnormality and consequent suffering.

But the ideal is the evolution of the attempted. Jesus recognizes the sociability of men, not merely as a condition of the new and divine age, but as the capacity that underlies the development of sinful men into a sanctified and normal brotherhood. In other words, man's capacity

[1] Luke 16 : 22 *sq.*

for union with other beings is the hope of his regeneration. It would lead too far afield to develop this conception of the dynamic forces of society as it deserves. The main thing to emphasize at present is the recognition by Jesus of this characteristic in the man but imperfectly righteous. He as well as the ideal man is a social personality. It is not merely in the glorious age to come that men are to be brethren, it is in the present evil age as well. " One is your Master," he declared in one of his most searching charges to the little band of disciples, "and all ye are brethren." [1] It is no mere happy choice of words that gave to those who attempted to incorporate his teachings this name. Altruism, self-sacrifice, was the constant lesson Jesus taught his followers. The sons of Zebedee, overambitious to monopolize the glories of the kingdom, the other ten who murmured quite as much from jealous disappointment as with indignation at their comrades' zeal, are bidden to serve rather than be served.[2] In the new order that was to be worked out upon the earth men were to be neighbors[3] and brothers. To exclude a man from the companionship of such was to reduce him

[1] Matt. 23: 8.   [2] Matt. 20: 20–28; Mark 10: 35–45.
[3] Luke 10: 25–37.

to the lowest social grade the Jewish vocabulary could describe.[1] To enter into brotherhood and sonship was the first step toward a future perfection.

VI

Thus from whatever point of view we examine the Christian conception of man, we find it including a capacity for union. And this union is not thought of by Jesus as one of mere collocation. It is essential to the truest life. To avoid it is to become abnormal and sinful. Out from the picture of a possible human life presented by his own living we gain a corroboration of his words to his followers. He himself was a social being. On the one side he was joined with physical forces, but on the other lay the needed sonship with God and fellowship with men. If we omit all doctrinal formulas it is nevertheless clear that in this teaching and its exemplification by Jesus, we have a presentation of humanity that must condition all theological and sociological statements that claim to be Christian. Further than this, there is gained a point of departure for the interpretation of less obvious teachings. If the Christian conception of man

[1] Matt. 18: 17, "The gentile and the publican."

is thus that of a social being that finds his complete life only in losing it in the life of others, we have as the Christian conception of society that of a necessary thing — that of an entity that is the complex not merely of physical environments but of personal as well. All unions that are the promptings of normal human instincts are therefore natural and helpful. All separations that are approved by such instincts are equally natural and necessary. And what is of especial significance, a Christian sociology becomes possible and necessary as the complement of a Christian theology.

CHAPTER III

To speak of Jesus as anticipating a regenerate society may appear to some as savoring of literalism and to others as a mere modernizing of the simple records of the gospels. Both objections would not be altogether without foundation. There is constant danger that, in the attempt to restate the teachings of Jesus in the terms of to-day's thought, exposition may wait too subserviently upon desire. The first century, albeit surprisingly like the nineteenth, was nevertheless not the nineteenth, and Jesus the Jew was not a product of Greek syllogisms and German hypotheses. Nevertheless, were one to come to the words of Jesus unbiassed by traditional interpretations, the impression would be inevitable that the goal of his efforts was the establishment of an ideal society quite as much as the production of an ideal individual. At any rate so his audiences thought. They sometimes sought to make him a leader of a revolution; sometimes they endeavored to pre-empt the chief offices in the future state. At one time they hailed him as the successor of David and carried him in triumph to the Temple; while in the hopes of his followers the chief significance of his return from the tomb and his newly revealed life lay at first in the possibility of revolution and the reëstablishment of a puissant Hebrew kingdom.[1]

That Jesus did not yield more completely to some of the efforts made by his hearers to hurry the realization of these hopes is less a testimony to their misunderstanding than to his own sagacity. And even if one does not choose to lay much stress upon these early guesses at the thought of Jesus, is it altogether without significance that he so uniformly speaks of himself as the Son of Man?[2]

[1] John 6 : 15; Matt. 20 : 21; Mark 11 : 10; Acts 1 : 6. In this connection the charge brought against Jesus before Pilate (Luke 23 : 2-5) as well as the famous conversation of John 18 : 33-38 deserve consideration. Beyschlag (*Neutestamentliche Theologie*, I., 155) in this connection has a couple of pregnant sentences as a sort of introduction to his study of the church.

[2] The use of this term by Jesus can hardly be said to commit him to a conception of humanity as an organism of which he was the typical exponent. Such an interpretation is attractive but less easily supported than that which sees in the expression one that had already a partially recognized Messianic content among the Jews (*cf.* Dan. 7 : 13 and *Book of Enoch*). By using it Jesus connected him-

But we are not left to conjecture or *a priori*
argument.   Jesus himself has chosen as his term
for the highest good [1] (or at least for one of the
prerequisites of its attainment) one that in itself
suggests social relations — the kingdom of God.[2]
No other term, unless it be Son of Man, is so
characteristic of Jesus; none is more certainly his.
Early Christianity, it is true, soon displaced it with
the more concrete term "church," and later Christianity has not hesitated to confound the two; but
with Jesus there was neither the substitution nor
the confusion.   Throughout the gospel sources
whether of the synoptic or the Johannine [3] cycle,
the usage is constant.   The kingdom is the goal
of effort, the reward of persecution, and the abode
of blessedness.

self with the current Messianic hopes, but in so veiled a way as to prevent a hasty acceptance of himself by the people as a leader of revolt.

[1] For a justification of this term see Matt. 13 : 44, 45.   See also
Issel, *Die Lehre vom Reiche Gottes im Neuen Testament*, p. 52 *sq.*

[2] Or kingdom of heaven.   For present purposes the distinction
between the two terms is unessential.   The content of each is the
same, although there are doubtless subjective if not critical grounds
for the use of each in different accounts.   See Wendt, *Teaching of
Jesus*, I., 370 n.

[3] In the few cases in which it is used.   In the Johannine teaching the idea of eternal life seems to have replaced that of the kingdom.   It is at least emphasized as the prerequisite of entrance into
the kingdom.   John 3 : 3, 5, 15, 16.   See Wendt, *Teaching of Jesus*,
I., 174, 242 *sq.*, 403 *sq.*

If any weight is to be given to the teachings of
Jesus, it is imperative that the meaning of this
term as he used it should be accurately gauged;
and it is characteristic of to-day's theological
thought that, alike from its Christocentric tendency and from its mastering desire for the
purely objective presentation of New Testament
teachings, it should especially seek to discover and
expound the "mysteries of the kingdom" as the
centre of all essentially Christian doctrine. The
effect of such exposition has been felt almost as
much in the realm of dogmatics and apologetics
as in that of biblical theology, but as much as in
either within the circle of earnest searchers after
a philanthropy and politics that shall be at once
scientific and Christian.[1]

[1] "No one can read attentively many modern theological works
without observing that the kingdom of God occupies a much more
prominent place in them than it has in the writings of former times.
This is partly due to the fact that scholars of the present day are
more careful to preserve the genuine historical ideas of other ages
and peoples instead of casting them into the forms or moulds of
later thought. . . . It is not merely an old Jewish form of thought,
which it is useful to study for the elucidation of the biblical literature . . . it is regarded by many as the most natural and ade-
quate conception that we can take to guide us in forming a system
of Christian theology. Further this notion of the kingdom of God
has not merely a speculative but a practical bearing; it is an idea
that craves to be realized in fact, or rather, it is not merely an idea
but a great reality, which has not yet fully attained its perfection,

I

If investigation in regard to Christ's conception of the individual's ideal state was hampered by the scarcity of data, the difficulties in the present case result from their abundance.[1] In one way this is extremely fortunate. Jesus never formally defines the term, and we are left to the discovery of that which is common in its usage. Naturally the investigator congratulates himself that the scope of his search is large. Yet the wealth of material is not without its drawbacks. A term thus frequently used will of necessity express at various times and in different connections different shades of thought. To discover the substance that lies behind this varying usage and is common to it all is no small task.

It is easy to discover that Jesus does not mean a merely political kingdom, or theocratic state. It is as easy for political enthusiasts to-day as it was in his own time to mistake here.[2] There are some

but in the perfecting of which men's help and labor may and should be employed." — Candlish, *The Kingdom of God*, pp. 2–3. These words are even truer to-day than when written eleven years ago.

[1] There are 106 passages in the gospels that contain references to the kingdom ; 50 occur in Matthew, 15 in Mark, 38 in Luke, 3 in John. Many of these, however, are parallel.

[2] As do some of the Christian Socialists. See for a brief account,

of Christ's statements that will bear a political interpretation, but they will also and indeed more naturally support another. Here, as always in dealing with language not containing formal definitions, it is necessary to canvass the entire field before recording decisions. He is indeed a singular exegete who discovers in either the early or the later language of Jesus anything that savors only of revolution or constitutional propaganda. The progress made by Jesus in the exposition of his mission does not consist in the erection of an eschatology out of the ruins of political hopes. At the beginning of his career he refuses the tempting suggestion to become a new Cæsar;[1] later his disciples are warned against "the leaven of Herod"[2] — that is of an overweening political ambition; he flees from those who would force him into politics,[3] and the Roman Pilate has no difficulty in convincing himself that in his extraordinary prisoner he has the opposite of Barabbas the revolutionist.[4]

Nor does Jesus use the term kingdom of God as figure of speech merely to indicate a perfect

the article on Christian Socialism in the *American Journal of Sociology*, I., 62. Wendt, *Teaching of Jesus*, I., 364 *sq.*, has an admirable critique of this view.

[1] Matt. 4 : 8–10 ; Luke 4 : 5–8. [3] John 6 : 15.

[2] Mark 8 : 15 ; *cf.* Mark 10 : 42. [4] John 18 : 33–38.

method of life for the individual.[1]   While of
course it was not without ethical content, the
term is not a mere synonym for personal holiness
or righteousness.   Indeed, there is but one saying
of Jesus [2] that in any way lends support to the
view that he thought of the kingdom as a subjective state of the individual, and even that can
hardly be used as a basis upon which to build
an individualistic system of self-culture.   It is
true that Jesus repudiates any grossly materialistic conception of his kingdom.   It is not to be
achieved by the ordinary means of world-rulers.[3]
It certainly is not to be established by the sword.[4]
Properly defined, it is spiritual.   But men are its
members, entering into it, or if unworthy, rejected
and cast out from it.   In the thought of Jesus it
is a kingdom, not a congeries of kingdoms as

[1] See Tolstoi, *The Kingdom of God is within You.*

[2] Luke 17 : 20, 21, where it is very likely, judging from the context, that the expression ἐντὸς ὑμῶν is used as rhetorically equivalent
to ἐν μέσῳ ὑμῶν.   With either interpretation it need not of necessity refer to a subjective appropriation of the kingdom.   Jesus would
hardly have credited his opponents (to whom the words were addressed) with the possession of the kingdom of God — especially
as we know he more than once charges them with the opposite
(John 8 : 44).   Taken in a collective sense the words are very
natural : The kingdom was in the midst of the Jews in the persons of
Jesus and his disciples.

[3] Matt. 4 : 8; *cf.* Matt. 11 : 12.   [4] John 18 : 36.

numerous as there are God-fearing men. If Paul
in one instance[1] seems to speak as if it were a
discipline, — "not eating and drinking, but righteousness and peace and joy in the Holy Ghost,"
—it is because his readers can be trusted to recognize the boldness of the metonymy. Jesus never
so speaks. With him ethical teachings are expressed explicitly and literally by such terms as
"perfect,"[2] "righteousness,"[3] and the like. In
one case he is reported as making righteousness
and the kingdom as coördinate goods,[4] but we
do not find in his words taken altogether justification for the closely allied conception that "the
kingdom is the rational idea of the chief good"[5]
which "can by no means be identified with the
universal moral society which is being developed
in the world."[6] While there is in these words a
gratifying recognition of the supreme position
accorded by Jesus to the kingdom, and while
such a view emphasizes what is certainly a dominant teaching of his, namely, that the highest

[1] Rom. 14 : 17.

[2] Matt. 5 : 48 ; 19 : 21.

[3] Matt. 3 : 15 ; 5 : 6, 10 ; *cf.* John 16 : 8, 10.

[4] Matt. 6 : 33.

[5] Kaftan, *The Truth of the Christian Religion*, II., 377.

[6] Kaftan, II., 379. J. Weiss (*Die Predigt Jesu vom Reiche
Gottes*, p. 64) deals rather summarily with Kaftan's views.

good consists in entering the kingdom, it is as
certainly doing violence to some of the analogies
that furnish much of the content of its definition
when the kingdom is made altogether supra-mun-
dane.   Many of the figures and words employed
by Jesus [1] in speaking of this " Highest Good "
show that he regarded it as by no means merely a
super-sensuous, super-rational postulate of morality
" which has the kingdom of moral righteousness
on earth as its intra-mundane correlative." [2]

It is doubtless true that, with Jesus, the term
filled the same office as some rational postulate
that is the dominant conception of any modern
philosophy.   But the identification of the content
of the two dominant thoughts is dangerous.   It is
one thing to appreciate the exact position of Jesus,
and it is quite another to translate it into the terms
of one's own philosophy.   The first step is one
of interpretation and must always condition the
second.   The chief criticism of this appropriation
of the kingdom as the capstone of a philosophy is
the same that must be passed upon so much of
the work of the theologian — it is attractive, it is
doubtless in the main true, but it is not the
thought of Jesus.   With him the kingdom was

[1] See for instance Matt. 13 : 38 *sq*.
[2] Kaftan, II., 366.

not a subjective but a concrete, objective reality : one that could be expected and enjoyed, if not here and now, at any rate in another world and age.

When thus we have rejected as incomplete these two conceptions, the one the gift of economic and the other of philosophical zeal for Christian truth, we have to deal with a very simple alternative. Did Jesus think of this concrete, objective kingdom of God as an eschatological or as a present reality ? Was it, with him, to use current expressions, heaven, or was it society ? Upon the answer given to this question will depend one's conception of the kingdom as purely religious or as both religious and social.

There is much that is worthy of consideration in the view that the use of the word by Jesus meant a Messianic millennium to be enjoyed by the righteous after death, or after the coming of a new age. On the historical side there may be urged the very conservative argument that Jesus "lived and spoke within the circle of eschatological ideas which Judaism had developed more than two hundred years before ; but he controlled them, by giving them a new content, and forcing them into a new direction."[1] On the exegetical it may be

[1] Harnack, *History of Dogma*, I., 62.

E

even more forcibly argued that "the kingdom of
the Messiah is the actual consummation of the
prophetic idea of the rule of God," and that the
term kingdom of God and kindred expressions
"never signify anything else than the kingdom
of the Messiah, even in those passages where they
appear to denote the (invisible) church, the moral
kingdom of the Christian religion, and such like,
or to express some modern abstraction of the concrete conception which is one given in the history." [1] While the historical and exegetical spirit
when once touched with the glow of religious
feeling can say: "We await no kingdom of God
which is to descend from heaven upon the earth
and destroy this world; but we hope to be
assembled with the church of Jesus Christ in the
heavenly $\beta a \sigma \iota \lambda \epsilon i a$. In this sense can we yearn
and say as did the ancient Christians: "Thy
kingdom come." [2]

The worth of each of these grounds for holding
to an apocalyptic and eschatological conception of
the kingdom is considerable, but especially can one

[1] Meyer, *Commentary on Matthew*, 3 : 2. For excellent statement of the similar views of Schmoller and J. Weiss, as well as the
opposing views of Ritschl, see the mediating article of Schneder-
mann in *Neue Kirchliche Zeitschrift*, 1894, No. 7, an abstract of
which appears in *The Thinker*, January, 1895.

[2] J. Weiss, *Die Predigt Jesu vom Reiche Gottes*, p. 76.

appreciate the historical position. Probably the recognition of the importance of the apocalyptic literature in the formation of the early Christian vocabulary, if not Christology, may yet be still further emphasized. Nor can it be denied that, especially in the latter part of his life, Jesus often used expressions [1] which, were they the only ones he had left, would be sufficient to justify the sweeping statement [2] that "the gospel entered into the world as an apocalyptic eschatological message, apocalyptical and eschatological not only in its form, but in its contents." But notwithstanding all this, the total impression made by the statements of Jesus in regard to the kingdom is not that of a post-mortem or post-catastrophic condition. At the outset of his preaching he announced its approach; [3] in the synagogue at Nazareth he declared the glowing promises of Isaiah fulfilled in the ears of his hearers; [4] unbelieving and hostile professional religious teachers were told that there was no longer need of straining after a glimpse of

[1] For instance, Luke 13 : 28 *sq.*; Mark 9 : 1; Matt. 25 : 31 *sq.*

[2] Harnack, *History of Dogma*, I., 58. — In the sentence next to that quoted, however, "apocalyptical" is given so broad a definition as to modify the force of this statement, and a few pages later (I., 62) the author gives what appears like a hesitating assent to the belief in a present kingdom.

[3] Mark 1 : 15.   [4] Luke 4 : 17–21.

a distant glory, for the kingdom was among them;[1] his followers are congratulated on seeing that for which their ancestors had longed, but had not seen;[2] the kingdom in the person of its members was already the good seed in the field, that is the world,[3] some of these members having had to struggle mightily in order to gain their entrance;[4] and the word of the kingdom is described as having different results in the hearts of different men.[5] The natural force of some of these passages may be evaded, but it is impossible in the light of them all and of other sayings of Jesus to believe that he occupied an exclusively eschatological point of view.   Only on one or the other of two alternatives can the opposite opinion be supported: Either Jesus saw the impossibility of his early plans for social or political revolution and looked to a heavenly Messianic kingdom, or such passages as are not clearly eschatological are to be rejected as the mistaken reports and interpretations of the gospel history.   But so far as the last possibility is concerned the contrary is quite as likely;[6] while in regard to the first suggestion, it may be replied

[1] Luke 17 : 20 *sq.*   [3] Matt. 13 : 24–43.

[2] Luke 10 : 23.   [4] Matt. 11 : 12–15.

[5] Mark 4 : 3 *sq.*; *cf.* Matt. 13 : 3 *sq.*

[6] Especially in the case of the apocalyptic elements in the discourses of Mark 13 and Matt. 24 and 25 where it has been suggested

that an unbiassed chronology and exegesis fail to disclose any such change on the part of Jesus. And finally, the apparent contradiction, or at least variation in the presentation of the kingdom, as invisible and yet seen, as future and yet present, may be naturally explained as indicating first, that Jesus thought of the kingdom as a concrete reality rather than an idea, and second, that this reality was not to be left as an unattainable ideal, but was to be progressively realized, perhaps evolved.

The question, however, yet remains. If we are thus led to reject as incomplete such interpretations of this term of Jesus as would restrict it to politics, or character, or heaven, can we hope to discover an approximate definition which shall combine the elements of truth each can be seen to contain and yet be consonant with the general course of the thought of Jesus?[1]

that a Jewish Apocalypse may have been combined with the words of Jesus.

[1] Were it desirable to take the space, it would be possible to give more fully the exegetical process by which the above definitions are rejected and another suggested. It may, perhaps, not be out of place to add a few representative authorities, whose definitions favor the social content. The author of *Ecce Homo* distinctly calls the kingdom of God a divine society (p. 48). Bruce (*Kingdom of God*, p. 46) thus summarizes possible interpretations : " It signifies some form of divine dominion. Abstractly reviewed, it might

II

By the kingdom of God Jesus meant an ideal (though progressively approximated) social order in which the relation of men to God is that of sons, and (therefore) to each other, that of brothers.

denote the reign of the Almighty over all creation through the operation of natural law ; or of the moral Governor of the world rendering to every man and nation according to their works ; or of the God of Israel ruling over a chosen people, and bestowing on them power, peace, and felicity as the reward of obedience to his divine will. Or it might mean something higher than any of these things, the highest form of dominion conceivable, the advent of which is emphatically fit to be the burden of a Gospel, viz., the reign of divine love exercised by God in his grace over human hearts believing in his love, and constrained thereby to yield him grateful affection and devoted service." He further quotes with approval the words of Keim (*Jesu von Nazara*, p. 54) : "Briefly stated, the religious heaven of Jesus meant the Fatherliness of God for men, the sonship of men for God, and the infinite spiritual good of the kingdom of heaven is Fatherhood and Sonship." Edersheim (*Life and Times of Jesus the Messiah*, I., 270) gives a characteristic definition of the term : " The rule of God, which was manifested in and through Christ is apparent in the church, gradually develops amidst hinderances; is triumphant at the second coming of Christ; and finally, perfected in the world to come." Stead (*Kingdom of God*, p. 69) regards it as " the fellowship of souls, divine and human, of which the law and life are love, wherein the Fatherhood of God and the Brotherhood of man as both are embodied in Jesus the Christ, are recognized and realized." Weiss (*Biblical Theology of the New Testament*, I., 63) does not accurately define the term as used by Jesus, but gives an approximate definition as follows : " What this kingdom of God is, is nowhere expressly said; the idea

The point of departure for any interpretation of the term must be the historical expectation of the Jews in the days of Jesus. What that expectation was is now pretty accurately known.[1] If all necessary allowance is made, on the one hand for the materialistic hopes of the masses, and on the other for the completed eschatology of the later

is regarded as one quite familiar to the people. In fact, no one in Israel, which was from the first to be a kingdom whose supreme Lord and King was Jehovah, could thereby understand anything else than a kingdom in which the will of God is fulfilled as perfectly upon earth as by the angels in heaven." Candlish (*Kingdom of God*, p. 197) gives what "may be taken as a basis at least for an exposition of the idea: The gathering together of men, under God's eternal law of righteous love, by the vital power of his redeeming love in Jesus Christ, brought to bear upon them through the Holy Spirit." Beyschlag (*Neutestamentliche Theologie*, I., 41) declares that "the kingdom of God is wherever the will of God is done on earth as in Heaven ; that is, where it is observed in an ideal manner. Accordingly . . . the kingdom is that ideal condition to which mankind and the world's history shall arrive, when God according to his inmost being, as eternal spirit and sacred love, shall be the all-filling and the all-conditioning element in the world." Denney (*Studies in Theology*, pp. 175-176) regards the kingdom as "a separate society in the world, in which there is a real union of persons who are conscious that they have what binds them to each other and separates them from the world ; but there is nothing formal or institutional about it." An even more concrete definition is given by those who identify a moral community with the kingdom; *e.g.*, Ritschl, Issel, Nitsch.

[1] Lütgert, *Das Reich Gottes nach den Synoptischen Evangelien*, ch. i.; Schürer, *The Jewish People in the Time of Jesus Christ*, Div. II., Vol. II., p. 170 *sq.*

Jewish writers, it will appear that the kingdom which was awaited was a new and divine Israelitish state, of which the Messiah, as the representative of God, was to be the head; all Jews, the members; and all peoples, the subjects. Palestine was to be the seat of its capital; the righteousness of the Jew, the qualification of membership. It was as intensely national as the proud spirit of a nation that remembered a Solomon and a Judas Maccabæus, and whose Jah was the only God, could imagine and describe under the smart of the Idumean and the Roman. To exhaust its glories was not within the power of literal language, and apocalypse and prophecy could but faintly foretell the glories of the new age and kingdom. No Jew thought of it as an abstract ideal. The proclamation of its approach by the people's preacher as he came in prophetic guise to the wilderness of Judea and summoned all to the washing of repentance, never would have so thrilled a nation had it been the ghostly thing announced by so many later Johns. It was as real as the men who sought to join it through repentance and renewed lives. The eternal religious influence of the Jew has lain not in his capacity to see the abstract in the concrete, the general in the specific, but in his noble genius for a rational anthropo-

morphism — the sight and the proclamation of
the Invisible in that which his senses revealed
to him. And his idea of the kingdom of God
was no sweet Greek dream of a past Golden
Age, but an intoxicating belief in a new state in
which righteousness was to reign and his enemies
were to bow before the Anointed of Jehovah.
His hope for the future was for an everlasting
Jerusalem that was to descend from heaven,
arrayed like a bride for her bridegroom, as free
as God's own realm. Even when the new kingdom grew more remote, and the hopelessness of
a tranquil realization of its sway grew weak, the
Jew never thought of it as anything but social.
Its members might have passed through a resurrection, and have survived the fearful woes that
ushered in its glories, but they were yet members
of a kingdom, inseparable from each other and
from the Messiah.

It was with the approaching fulfilment of this
undefined expectation of an actual, concrete,
though divine, political society, that Jesus began
his preaching. He took the hope as he found
it. He never needed to define it. He had
simply to correct and elevate the immanent idea.
The Christian kingdom is the Jewish kingdom,
but transfigured and made universal by the clari-

fications of Jesus. Membership in it is no longer
to be a matter of birth. The "children of the
kingdom" were to know that the despised Gentile might enter in before them. Thus it is that,
although Jesus sometimes refers especially to
the dominion of God in his kingdom, he generally
keeps prominent the social conception.

And as a new social order the kingdom of God
had really begun to be appreciable if only men
would so believe. It was among them;[1] the
divine benefactions of Jesus were evidence that
it had come upon them;[2] the unworthy hamlet
that refused the entrance of its heralds was yet
to know that in rejecting them it had rejected
the object of its hopes.[3] And the analogies with
which this present and appreciable kingdom is
described are full of social signification. As in
its very genesis the term denoted social relations,
so is it a net,[4] a great feast,[5] a family,[6] into each
of which men enter and from which they may
be excluded. Its members are seeds scattered
over the field of the world; its enemies are the
tares sown by the king's enemy.[7] For so true

[1] Luke 17 : 20.
[2] Matt. 21 : 28.
[3] Luke 10 : 10-12.
[4] Matt. 13 : 47-50.

[5] Luke 14 : 15 *sq.*
[6] Matt. 23 : 28; Luke 15 : 11-32.
[7] Matt. 13 : 24-30, 36-43.

is Jesus to the old terminology that he even re-
expresses with new force the conception of King
Messiah. He is this king,[1] and, to use the conventional imagery of the prophets, his coming in
supremacy is to be upon the clouds of heaven.[2]

This conclusion that by the kingdom of God
Jesus meant a society, is confirmed by the position which the kingdom, as the ideal, occupies in
relation to the world,[3] as the actual social order.
The world is not the demoniacal kingdom supposed by some scholars to have been established
by Satan as a sort of counterpart to the Messianic,
and from whose agents Jesus won a glorious
victory. Such a view finds little foundation in
the gospel records. Jesus does, indeed, argue
pointedly that his deeds of kindness cannot be
taken as substantiating his partnership with
Satan — "a kingdom cannot be divided against
itself."[4] But, even if it were possible to make
this the basis of a Christian demonology, it is

[1] Luke 22: 28 sq.

[2] Matt. 26: 64; Mark 13: 26. These apocalyptic sayings are here
used as those of Jesus. For a discussion of the possibly composite
character of the discourses, see Wendt, *Die Lehre Jesu*, I., 35 sq.

[3] ὁ κόσμος. It is hardly necessary to call attention to the fact
that in the English version of the New Testament "world" is the
translation of αἰών (age) as well.

[4] Mark 3: 22–27.

exposed to a suspicion of semi-accommodation on
the part of Jesus such as does not affect his use
of the term world.   By this word Jesus evidently meant the environment within which and
out of which his kingdom was to grow.   And
this environment is not merely physical, it is
social.   From it he chose his followers.[1]   To it,
as the ultimate bounds of their activity, his disciples were to go, from its members to win still
other subjects of the divine rule.[2]   In the midst
of its influences his followers were to be left,[3]
the light that should illumine it,[4] the salt that
should preserve it.[5]   In it, as in a great field, was
to be reaped the harvest of good and bad men.[6]
In the Johannine gospel we find this conception a
part of the very structure of the philosophy that
interprets the life of Jesus.   The world needed him
as a Saviour, and, because of God's love, received
him,[7] only to hate and reject him.[8]   And yet he
was its light, its life.[9]   Gradually, as the story of
the defeat of Jesus grows darker, its opposition is
more dwelt upon.   The world lost the vision of
its Saviour,[10] rejoiced at his departure,[11] hated and

[1] John 15 : 19.   [5] Matt. 5 : 13.   [9] John 8 : 12; 6 : 26 *sq*.
[2] Matt. 26 : 13.   [6] Matt. 13 : 38.   [10] John 14 : 19.
[3] John 17 : 15.   [7] John 3 : 16; 17 : 18.   [11] John 16 : 20.
[4] Matt. 5 : 14.   [8] John 3 : 19.

persecuted his followers.[1] That which should
have been full of a divine harmony grows discord-
ant, the abode of evil.

To all this the kingdom of Jesus stands in opposition. So far as this social environment is thus
evil, it could not account for the disciples, still less
for himself. Yet the contrast is helpful, for if the
one kingdom be social, so must also be the other.
Indeed, it is clear that Jesus foresaw that his ideal
society would be composed of members drawn
from the old. If, as it slowly grew in the midst of
such surroundings, it was to suffer, it nevertheless
was to be cheered by its founder's victory and
expect likewise to conquer[2] — if not in this age,
at least in the next. But its very conquest would
be thus that of a new over an old social order.
This is the substance of the vision in what is perhaps an early Christian emendation of a Jewish
apocalypse, "the kingdoms of the world are become the kingdom of our Lord and his Christ."[3]

It is in this contrast, also, that the general character of the new Christian social order is most
distinctly seen. The old is evil; the new is ideal.
The old is under a prince who is to be judged;[4]
the new is of God. The members of the one are

[1] John 15.: 19.　　　　　[3] Rev. 11 : 15.
[2] John 16: 33.　　　　　[4] John 16 : 8.

dominated by selfish ambition; those of the other
are not so to be, but are to seek greatness in
service.[1]   Within one there is to be found the
restless, anxious search for material goods;[2] within the other food and drink and dress are to be
provided by a loving Father as great but not the
greatest needs of the trustful soul.[3]   In a word,
in the old social order Jesus saw the tyranny of
selfishness and hatred; in the new, he sees a
universal reign of love — the fatherhood of God
and the brotherhood of men.

III

This expression, the fatherhood of God and
brotherhood of men, is in many minds the substance of Christianity.   And such is the case if
these terms are given their proper meaning.   But
at this point we have to distinguish sharply between two possible conceptions of divine sonship,
neither of which is inconsistent with Christian
doctrine.   On the one hand there is the noble sentiment that holds sway in most religious thought
to-day, according to which all men are the sons of
God in that they were created by him, possess
moral attributes, and are capable, however wicked,

[1] Matt. 20: 26–28; 23: 11; Mark 9: 35; 10: 43, 44; Luke 22: 26.
[2] Luke 12: 30.   [3] Luke 12: 30; Matt. 6: 31, 32.

of rising to nobility in self-sacrifice and devotion —
in a word, in that they possess simply by virtue
of their humanity an ineradicable likeness to God.
According to this view, God is always humanity's
loving Father, ready to forgive, and yearning after
his lost children.   On the other hand, there is the
more intensive conception of sonship, which, while
never denying that in a general sense men may be
spoken of as the sons of God, and affirming strenuously the love of God for men, yet uses the word
to express the more intimate and responsive relation with God actually enjoyed by those who are
seeking noble ends, who are consciously seeking
moral strength from prayer, who in a personal
sense love God while seeking to keep his com-
mandments, and who, through this personal contact with God, gain a new character, which, while
possessed of the same powers as before, is yet
fuller of the divine likeness.

These distinctions are evidently those of terminology rather than of thought and are based upon
different uses of words that, since the literal idea
of begetting a son is clearly impossible, must at
bottom express an analogy.   Whatever of mutual
love and similarity of nature is connoted by the
human relationship of son and father is used as the
best analogue for the relations of man and God.

These relations are regarded by the one party as already existent, and by the other as dependent upon regeneration. Yet the two positions are not exclusive. The man who especially emphasizes universal, racial divine sonship will be sure to admit widely different degrees of filial obedience and love; while, as already intimated, he who does not prefer to use thus indiscriminately the only words capable of supreme religious content, nevertheless is most eager to urge at the same time God's love for the race and the possibilities of reformation on the part of the evil man.[1] Neither party would of necessity disregard the punishment of sin, though giving it a greater or less prominence in their theological systems, according to the emphasis laid upon the justice or benevolence of God.

Of these two uses of the same terms, which was the one adopted by Jesus? The second and more restricted. Not that he denies that relationship of God and men which we moderns denote as the divine paternity and sonship. The most casual reading of the New Testament shows that this conception of the love of God is the very core

[1] The advocates of this view sometimes claim that God is always the Father of men, but that all men are not the sons of God — a use of terms which singularly confuses literal and analogical conceptions. It would be better to drop the figure altogether and substitute its content.

of the Christian teaching[1] of which Jesus was
himself the living revelation. It is not impossible,
though it is by no means beyond question, that
in the third of the three parables preserved by
Luke[2] he sets forth this love of God in the terms
of fatherhood. Further, it may be true, as Wendt[3]
says, that "he proceeds upon the certainty of it,
as upon an undoubted axiom."   But even with
these admissions, it seems certain that Jesus in
his positive teachings, with a characteristic sense
of that which is appropriate, reserved ever the
noblest words of humanity for designating the
noblest relations; that is, the relations of those
persons who were members of the kingdom of
God — who, to use the Johannine expression, had
been born anew.[4] Unless Jesus were to invent a
new vocabulary familiar terms must be used to
express his relationship, and what could be nobler
or more expressive than those which express the
more sacred and unselfish in human life? In fact,
he almost explicitly thus defined his words when
he repudiated physical relations and made those
his family who did the will of his Father in

[1] Matt. 6: 31 *sq.*; Luke 18: 14; Matt. 18: 14 ; 5: 44, 48.
[2] Luke 15: 3-32.   [3] *Teaching of Jesus*, I., 199.
[4] John 3: 3.   If the other less likely, though possible translation of ἄνωθεν "from above" be adopted, the expression gains in
explicit reference.

F

heaven.[1]   This appears also in the Johannine
comment upon the significance of Jesus, "As
many as received him, to them gave he power
to become the children of God."[2]   From the
exactness of these statements one cannot help
concluding that to extend the use of these terms
of Jesus to all mankind is to confound what was
in his mind a possible condition with that which
was real only in the case of far too small a
number.   It would probably also be true to his
conception to say that the terms son and father
in the ethical sense — which was the only force he
gave them except that of purely physical relationship — are correlative, the one relationship not existing without the other.[3]   But it is not a question
of abstract ethics that here concerns us, but of fact.
And the fact of a real spiritual union with God, the
outcome of man's natural and normal powers, in
default of better terms is described by Jesus and
the earlier Christian writers as a sonship and a
fatherhood.

It may be urged that the point at issue is
trivial.   If Jesus recognizes and enforces that universal love of God for men which is to-day denoted

[1] Matt. 12: 49, 50 ;   Mark 3: 34, 35 ;   Luke 8: 21.
[2] John 1 : 12.
[3] See Wendt, *Teaching of Jesus*, I., 191, 199.

by the expression fatherhood of God, and that moral nature and possibility in man that we judge to imply the divine image; and if, indeed, his use of the words themselves is simply a question of terminology, why attempt any sharp discrimination? What does it signify if, while teaching to-day's doctrine of the universal fatherhood of God, he prefers to limit the extent of words and to call only the members of the new society brothers one of another and sons of God?

The answer is threefold. To give to a specific term a general meaning is to confuse all a man's teaching. That which is true of the divine paternity in the sense of Jesus, is not true of the divine paternity in the larger sense. Promises made to those who in this deeper sense pray to their Father are not to be transferred to those who will not so pray, but prefer hatred to love, wickedness to purity. A bad man cannot honestly desire that the Father's kingdom should come and that his will should be done on earth as in heaven. A man full of selfishness and licentiousness cannot seek first the kingdom of God and his righteousness in firm trust that a heavenly Father will provide for his necessities. The example of a merciful heavenly Father is hardly sufficient to move a cruel and rapacious man to deeds of

love. As a result, therefore, to extend the usage
of Jesus farther than the limits he himself has
set, is to contravene one of the fundamental distinctions of his teachings: the eternal distinction
between goodness and badness. A bad man can
become a good man — even in his wickedness he
is loved by God; but he must attempt to realize
his nobler possibilities, he must begin to be a good
man before Jesus will call him a son of God. We
may not ourselves prefer such a terminology, but
if we are to represent Jesus we must use words
as he used them — and few indeed have been the
teachers who, by a reservation of common terms,
have expressed more accurately an ethical distinction so fundamental. But further, upon this ideal
sonship is based the ideal brotherhood. Men are
brothers through the possession of a life derived
from the same parent. So in the new social order
of Jesus, those men who have satisfied the deepest
possibilities of their nature and are living in union
with God — that is, are righteous — are brothers.
Here again we meet with an accurate use of terms.
The members of the kingdom alone are called
brothers by Jesus.[1] Outside of those that clearly

---

[1] Wendt (*Teaching of Jesus*, I., 337) holds to the opposite but
admits that "Jesus has nowhere in his recorded utterance expressly
given a universality of extent to this idea of brother."

refer to physical relationship there is not a saying
of Jesus preserved for us that does not restrict
this most expressive term to the description of this
new social relationship, the possibility and nature
of which it was his mission to reveal. In actual
society as he saw it, fraternal relations were not
prevalent. Men quarrelled, lusted, hated, deceived,
fought. Their very philanthropy [1] and religion [2]
were tinged with selfishness. But in the new
social order he sought to portray and inaugurate
none of these things were to be. Men were to
be perfect as their heavenly Father was perfect,[3]
and among them reconciliation, purity, love, were
to be the outcome of their consciousness of their
divine brotherhood. And what is this but saying
that the ideal society that awaits the world as a
fulfilment of man's social capacities is no mere
collocation of dissimilar, repellent individuals, but
a union of men similarly righteous, all alike possessed of a consciousness of noble possibilities,
seeking the good one of another, with moral impulses springing from their religious life — a unity
whose bonds are organic and spiritual ?

[1] Matt. 6 : 2 ; *cf.* Luke 14: 12 *sq.*
[2] Matt. 6 : 5, 16.
[3] Matt. 5 : 48.

IV

Such, then, is in essence the ideal social order of Jesus — a divine brotherhood. It is necessary now to reëxamine his words in order to discover whether or not they have any practical bearing upon to-day's social life.   Does Jesus regard this ideal as a Utopia, an idealist's heaven which is to hang forever over the world an unattainable dream?   Or does he think of it as at least partly realizable in human life?

It is at once evident that Jesus does not regard this new social order as isolated.   Some time it will embrace all the earth.   In this particular he both follows and enlarges the idea of the kingdom of God as he found it.   It is not therefore a school or brotherhood in the narrow sense of academy or monastery that he founded, but a social force capable of expressing itself in a universal society.

It is also clear that the new society may be very widely distributed.   The bond of union is not that of organization, but that of a common relation to the King and Father.   Distance is therefore not an element adverse to a progressive social unity whose unity is not that of a circumference but of radii.   Jesus himself in his own estimation is the visible expression of the centre in which all relations converge and unite. In his death he drew all men to himself.[1] Wherever a little group of brethren is, there is also the Son of Man.[2] The parable of the leaven[3] indicates at once a diffused and growing unity.

All this points to a spiritual element in the character of the new society. It is not to be a mere coercive aggregation of men; its essential element is not its form but the coördinating and unifying spiritual life that is common to all. Membership is psychical, not external, and its blessings are also spiritual. The poor in spirit[4] are to be its members; within it the mourner is to be comforted;[5] those hungry for righteousness are to be fed;[6] the poor cared for,[7] perplexed and worrying souls reassured,[8] the pure in heart to see God.[9] The Johannine conception is even more explicit. Entrance to it is dependent wholly upon a spiritual renewal,[10] and in the sonship thus obtained are the forces[11] that are to make for the complete realization of the specific ideals Jesus presents as the features of the perfect social life. In this spiritual character of the kingdom lie its

[1] John 13: 32.
[2] Matt. 18: 20.
[3] Matt. 13: 33.
[4] Matt. 5: 3.
[5] Matt. 5: 4.
[6] Matt. 5: 6.
[7] Matt. 6: 24 *sq*.
[8] Matt. 6: 31, 32.
[9] Matt. 5: 8.
[10] John 3: 3.
[11] John 15: 1, 4.

energy and its practicability. Membership within it is possible for all since all are spiritual.[1] It can move not merely in organized but in unorganized ways. It can remake alike the ambition of one of its members and public opinion and social conceptions. In a word it is dynamic — a power as well as a condition. And this power lies within the new possibilities of divine sonship.

In its turn this points to the possibility of a beginning and progressive social order here and now. Jesus in his double revelation of God to man and humanity to man inaugurated its historical life.[2] If consciousness of sonship is possible for men, and moral development along both individual and social lines is made possible by man's very constitution; if Jesus could speak of his immediate disciples as enjoying the blessings of the kingdom [3] and as brethren with God as their Father; and if the number of these followers was to increase numerically just as their virtue might deepen, — the conclusion seems unavoidable that a "divine society" is thought of by Jesus as already within the world. Its spiritual elements save it

[1] Matt. 8 : 11.

[2] In the full Christian meaning of the term. This is not to deny a pre-Christian history of the kingdom of God. See Bestmann, *Enstehungsgeschichte des Reiches Gottes*, Vol. I.

[3] Matt. 11 : 11, 12 ; *cf.* Luke 17 : 21 and Matt. 12 : 28.

from the limbo of Utopias. True, it is not yet
complete, either intensively or extensively. In its
social as in its individual aspect the progress of
righteousness is gradual, first the blade, then the
ear, then the full corn in the ear.[1] But Jesus was
no believer in a dualism either in heaven or on
earth, and this regenerate society in the world is
slowly to spread until, like yeast in the dough, it
transforms its entire environment. To use the
noble words of an early Christian writer, "What
the soul is in the body that are Christians in the
world."[2]

The method and the means by which the world
is thus to be transformed into the kingdom do not
concern us here. It is enough to point out the
fact that the kingdom is thought of by Jesus as
present as well as future, and that its history is an
evolution. Each stage of the growth will be to
a considerable degree determined by the character
of the men — or groups of men — with whom the
new order has to deal.[3] Naturally the rates of
progress will vary at different developing points.
The influence of the old social environment will
always be felt, and its elements will yield them-

[1] Mark 4: 28.   [2] *Epistle to Diognetus*, chap. vi.
[3] See the familiar parable of the sower, Matt. 13: 3 *sq.*; **Mark**
4: 3 *sq.*; Luke 8: 5 *sq.*

selves with unequal readiness to the new ideal.
But the process nevertheless will go on. According to Jesus, it will be remembered, men from
their very constitution, if only that constitution be
allowed its normal operations, will unite in some
social bond. To make this social bond religious
and social relationships moral is to bring in the
new order of things.

Historically speaking the stages thus involved
are, the appearance of Jesus, the formation of the
first group of men whom Jesus gathered as the
nucleus of future greatness, the gradual development of other similar groups of men throughout
the world, the gradual leavening of all social environment, the consummation of this process in
the new age.

What, then, is this consummation, this end of the
age? Certainly not death. Jesus seldom considers the death of the individual. The transition
between "this age" and "the coming" is between eras and societies. The glorious kingdom
is to come after the period of growth and conflict
is past. The catastrophic completion of the slow
process is after the possibilities of that process
are exhausted, and with it will begin a new and
better age.

It would not be safe to say that this is not to be

after death. From some of the words of Jesus it seems as if such were the case. But in this connection Jesus ignores death. He never for a moment thinks that men cease to be men simply because they are dead. No more does human society. But whether before or after death, the realization of this ideal to which the age has slowly been leading the race is certain. The time of conflict will pass. The power of the new order will be so great that all opposition will have passed or have been crushed. That for which men have prayed will appear. The kingdom will then in truth have come, and the will of God will be done as in heaven. Those who wilfully refuse to join in the society will grieve most miserably, their suffering being the result of their inability to share in the blessings of the new humanity.

Although this triumphant establishment of the ideal society is the goal of human evolution under the impulse of the newly revealed religious forces, Jesus does not allow himself to weaken the practical operation of an attempted realization of its laws by any over description of its joys. In fact, beyond general allusions in the way of warnings or exhortations, his concern with them is comparatively little. He was no Mahomet with alluring visions of a sensuous Paradise, or even a Sweden-

borg, with noble mysticism delighting to symbol-
ize the deepest truths of life.   He has, for instance,
much more to say about marriage and wealth than
about heaven and hell.   As may appear later,
his descriptions of what should be special social
relationships are never temporizing but absolute,
yet the consummation of the age's progress is chiefly
described as an incentive to approximate its ideal
conditions in the present.   In a word, Jesus con-
centrates his attention upon the period of development.   And this is the same thing as saying that
the nearest approach to a realization of a Christian
society is to be found where the principles of his
ideal society are most nearly expressed in the
institutions and life of a people, where this divine
sonship and the consequent human fraternity
become facts, not the premises of a doctrinaire
sociology.

Is, then, this new social order, as it develops in
scattered groups and attempts to transfigure the
world, coextensive with the life of the church ?

Jesus gives us no clear answer, but his position,
to judge from the few uncertain expressions of the
gospel,[1] seems to imply that the church is one
form of the attempt to realize the principles embodied in the kingdom of God.   But there is not

[1] Matt. 16: 18 ; 18: 17.

a trace of any belief on his part that the two would ever be coextensive. The new social order was to be religious; historically, it has made much progress through the aid of religious organizations. But it is as much grander than the church as an ideal is grander than the actual; as much wider as social life is wider than any one institution; as much more catholic as Christianity is more catholic than ecclesiasticism.[1]

V

Jesus, then, thinks that an ideal society is not beyond human attainment, but is the natural possibility for man's social capacities and powers. The new social order, as a spiritual fellowship between men and between God and men that expresses itself in social relations, may at once be established potentially in the midst of that other social order, which is based upon a disregard of the normal religious and social capacities of men, and which becomes of necessity self-destructive and in tendency anarchistic. In his conception of this progressively realized social order we see that two elements are essential: the divine sonship

[1] For an exceedingly well balanced discussion of this point see Denney, *Studies in Theology*, ch. viii. See also Fairbairn, *The Place of Christ in Modern Theology*, pp. 515–519; Orr, *The Christian View of God in the World*, especially, pp. 402–412; Freemantle, *The World as the Subject of Redemption*.

as seen in the moral regeneration of the individual; and the organic union of good men typified by the family. To describe in some detail the extension of these principles of sonship and brotherhood to the various phases and institutions of social life, and to show in what lie the forces that aid in their incarnation, must be left to subsequent chapters.

CHAPTER IV

THE FAMILY

IF society be the union of those who by nature demand social life, all its various phases will be expressions of this need of union. But this, as we have already seen, does not exhaust the social principles of Jesus. Humanity can be normally social only when it is fraternal. The ideal is not merely a union, but a union of brothers. And what is thus true of society in the aggregate is true also of its various institutions. There too must fraternity be the ideal and the test of normality. This principle is not hard to trace, but in some particulars it has singularly escaped attention. In nothing, however, is it more apparent than in Christ's teaching in regard to the family.

I

As one might expect *a priori*, the family is regarded by Jesus as one manifestation of the essential social character of men. The sexes complement one another as the two halves of a whole. This finds expression in his well-known use of the words and incidents of Genesis. Marriage has a divine origin. Husband and wife are joined together by God, so that they are no longer two but one. It is noteworthy that Jesus thus regards marriage as monogamous — not indeed as the result of an evolving conventionality, but as the result of the divine creative act.[1] Monogamy is thus regarded by him as the only normal, the only divine basis of family relations. By this reaffirmation of the noble social teaching of Moses,[2] Jesus sets his disapproval upon all forms of plural marriage, whether illegal or legal. In none of his teachings have we greater economy of expression, but in none is his meaning less in doubt.

But it would be an incomplete presentation of the position of Jesus to stop at this point. If we attempt to arrange his thought in any system, the union of two persons in marriage becomes one factor in the union of the race; a

[1] Matt. 19: 5, 6; Mark 10: 6–8. No words reported as those of Jesus are more certainly his than these concerning marriage and divorce.

[2] It should not be overlooked that in using the expression "twain" Jesus follows the Septuagint rather than the Hebrew, which reads simply "them."

union which appears at once natural for mankind, and also a symbol of that divine social
order which is to come, when all men are to be
sons of God and society thus a brotherhood.
Marriage is not the creature of law. Law can
simply recognize and protect it. With Jesus
on its physical side marriage is an actual union
of complementing personalities — a forming of
one flesh. It is one of the primal *facts* of
human life, and because it is a conditioning fact
and not a merely formal conception of the law-
books, it is especially sacred and inviolable. It
is in itself a fraternity — a microcosmic kingdom
of God.

On its physical side Jesus regards marriage —
like the other physical elements in the evolving
social order — as an institution to be found only
in the present æon. The much-married woman
of the Sadducees' riddle,[1] in the life beyond the
grave was no longer to be subject to the perplexing levirate law, for in the resurrection humanity
neither marries nor is given in marriage, but is
to be as the angels of heaven. And yet while
Jesus thus recognizes the physical basis of marriage, he never regards it as in any way sinful
or ignoble; so far is he removed from the perver-

---

[1] Matt. 22 : 23–30; Mark 12 : 18–25; Luke 20 : 27–36.

G

sions that an ascetic faith has so frequently forced upon humanity.[1] As long as human nature and human relations are as they are, so long will marriage be the first human tie. For it ties otherwise the closest are to be broken. Filial dependence, the family itself are to yield before the marital union and the future family. But it is altogether within the spirit of Jesus' teaching, although perhaps not to be derived from any of his recorded words, to say that the physical is not the only, nor by any means the permanent element in marriage. This must be found in the same fraternal spirit which guarantees a perpetuation of the kingdom. Just as this ideal society is independent of physical bounds and changing physical elements, so, we may infer, is the ultimate basis of the marriage relation to be found in spiritual rather than physical unity. Between man and wife there is to be a union in spirit that springs from a love that is not mere passion but is volitional and moral. When physical surroundings have passed away, when there is no longer need of this means of perpetuating the race, then will the spiritual union, which must have accompanied the physical, alone survive, and the ties of

[1] Nor is there a hint of the later Christian teaching that it is unwise for a widow or widower to remarry.

family become merged in those of the all-embracing fraternity, and the love and union of husband and wife transmuted into the love and union of children of a common Father.

Thus here, as in other social relations, if the family is to be a phase of the divine society, the spiritual union must supplement and ennoble the physical. "If trust be incomplete, marriage, we know, cannot have its perfect work. If trust be broken, marriage perishes. But by interchange of thought and hope and prayer in marriage, trust ripens into faith." [1]

It is unnecessary for the appreciation of this position of Jesus to follow him in his terminology. It is of little or no consequence whether the basis of this conception of the marriage relation be regarded as a literal divine word or as human nature itself; whether the institution itself be the outcome of a creative *fiat* or of evolution. The one essential point is its absolute truth from the point of view of both ethics and human history. Marriage is indeed a fundamental human relation; it is in its normal condition when monogamous; it is something more than a living together of man and woman; it is a psychical as well as a physical completion of individuals;

[1] Westcott, *The Social Aspects of Christianity*, p. 25.

and as such it is in the largest sense of the
term a fraternity that depends for its perpetuation upon love.[1]

II

From this point of view Christ's teaching in
regard to divorce becomes not only simple but
inevitable. So long as marriage is not a mere
matter of law or conventionality, but is one expression of the fundamental social nature of man
in both its physical and spiritual expression; and
so long as it is monogamous, to be characterized
by the modesty that is possible alone in such a
relation; so long must it be unbreakable by statute. Divorce by Jesus is regarded as impossible,
except as a formal recognition of an already
broken union. As marriage gives rise to an
actual union of personalities it can be broken
only by an actual severance of this union. When
this is not the case, law can no more annul it
than it can annul an arch. "What God hath
joined together let not man put asunder." In

---

[1] "It is clear that monogamy has long been growing innate in
the civilized man. For all the ideas and sentiments now associated
with marriage have, as their implication, the singleness of the
union." — Spencer, *Principles of Sociology*, I., 673. See also p.
752 where he declares such a marriage to be "manifestly the ultimate form." So Westermarck, *The History of Human Marriage*,
p. 510. Drummond, *The Ascent of Man* is here suggestive.

this again Jesus was in contrast with his times. The astonishing laxity which prevailed among the fashionable clique at Rome, even if all due allowance be made for the natural exaggeration of moralists and poets, is well known from the literature of the empire,[1] to say nothing of the early Christian writers.[2] But the same tendencies were at work among the less corrupt circles of Judea. There, too, the general laxity in regard to divorce was quite as striking. The liberal school of Hillel was here more the offender than that of Shammai. By an exceedingly broad interpretation of Deut. 24:1 (the sole ground for divorce in the Mosaic code), it was judged permissible to divorce a wife if she had spoiled her husband's dinner, and later, if we are to accept the words of R. Akiba, even if the husband discovered a woman more to his liking.[3] Jesus was in fact opposed by his countrymen, to whom, thanks to the popular teaching, his doctrine seemed fanaticism. Moses, they objected,[4]

[1] See Friedländer, *Sittengeschichte der Römer*, I., ch. 5; Döllinger, *The Gentile and the Jew*, II., 230 *sq.*

[2] See, for instance, Clement of Alexandria and Jerome.

[3] But there is here opportunity, as in the case of Juvenal, for a large allowance for rhetoric. Yet the general ease of divorce is undeniable. The Talmud devotes an entire tractate (*Gittin*) to the subject. (See Edersheim, *Life of Jesus the Messiah*, II., 332 *sq.*; Stern, *Die Frau im Talmud;* Weill, *La Femme Juive.*)

[4] Matt. 19:7.

had allowed divorce, had even commanded that a "bill of divorcement" should be given in case of separation. Jesus was not to be shaken from his position by any quotation of ancient authorities. He admitted that Moses had allowed divorce as an expedient, a choice between two evils, but, appealing not to statute but to life, he protested in words his hearers would have regarded as older even than the law of Moses, that such permission was in violation of a primary fact of human society, an undoing of the law of creation, a violation of human nature.

It is a little remarkable, but indicative of the importance Jesus accorded the family, that, not content with thus enunciating a general principle, he should have gone into minuter treatment of this one social relation. His position upon many subjects which are of burning interest to-day, and, to judge from the writings of the time, were often quite as much so in his own day, is often noncommittal, almost always reserved, although occasionally, as in the case of ceremonial uncleanness, he expresses in a pregnant sentence a specific principle. But in the matter of divorce he has left us some of the most explicit legislation the gospels have preserved. Under no circumstances, provided that the marriage union is not actually broken through the unfaithfulness of one of the parties, is a husband to divorce his wife, or a wife her husband.[1] In case there is no such actual breaking of the marriage tie, a husband who puts his wife away, be it never so legally, causes her to be judged as belonging to that class of women who have really given grounds for divorce; he brands her an adulteress.[2] If, on the basis of such divorce she should marry, both she and the new husband commit sin. The original union is still existent. Yet if adultery has actually been committed, the guilty party may be divorced.[3] In

---

[1] This addition is noteworthy. It had not been customary among the Jews for wives to divorce their husbands, although about the time of Jesus we meet several cases of its occurrence among the official class. Thus Salome, sister of Herod I., divorced her husband (Josephus, *Antiquities of the Jews*, 15 : 7 : 10), and later Herodias, at least nominally, divorced her husband Herod, in order to live with his brother, Herod Antipas. The Mishna also grants the wife the right of seeking divorce. *Yebumoth*, 65, a. b. *Cettubboth*, 77, a. But the custom was more Roman than Jewish.

[2] Matt. 5 : 32.

[3] This view presupposes the exceptive clause in Matt. 5 : 32 and 19 : 9. This position is not beyond question, especially since that clause does not appear in Mark 10 : 11, although Meyer may be correct in saying that it is there understood as a matter of course. It is also lacking in Luke 16 : 18, but the omission by Luke is not so serious as that by Mark. Wendt (*Teaching of Jesus*, I., 354) judges this omission as sufficient ground for the view that "the simple, unqualified statement ' to put away a wife on the ground of unchastity is not culpable adultery,' does not correspond with the

such a case it would appear as if the two parties became *de facto* unmarried; since their union is broken both in its physical and its psychical aspects, they are no longer one flesh, nor is theirs a community of love. They are not, therefore, forbidden by Jesus to marry again.[1]

But two things are here very evident: (1) Jesus

meaning of Jesus." That meaning is "that the obligation of marriage is absolute, and no dissolution of it is possible without incurring the guilt of adultery." And it must be admitted that on critical grounds the addition of the clause by Matthew (so Bleek, Weiss, Holtzmann, and others) is quite as probable as its omission by Mark. (Yet see Gould, *Critical and Exegetical Commentary on the Gospel according to Mark, in loco.*) Yet on the grounds stated in the text the exception does not appear foreign to the thought of Jesus. Even were the clause omitted, we should have very possibly a strong rhetorical statement like others of Jesus. (For example, Matt. 5 : 29, 30, 34.) And in any case the main thought of Jesus would be unaffected. An interesting commentary upon his position is to be seen in the interpretation put by Jesus upon the status of the much married Samaritan woman, John 4 : 18.

[1] See Hovey, *The Scriptural Law of Divorce*, and *Studies in Ethics and Religion*, p. 321 *sq.* and commentaries (especially Meyer, and Broadus) on the above passages. See also Strong, *Philosophy and Religion*, 431–442, and Woolsey, *Divorce and Divorce Legislation*, ch. 2, although so far as his interpretation of the teaching of Jesus on this point is concerned, President Woolsey's views were later reversed. (See the essay by President Strong just mentioned.) The church has not generally favored this interpretation. See Schmidt, *Social Results of Christianity*, p. 201 *sq.*, and, especially for the Roman Catholic position, Convers, *Marriage and Divorce*, and Pascal, "L'Association Catholique," *Revue des Questions Sociales et Ouvrières*, January, 1896.

does not command a divorce even in the most extreme cases. His recognition of the possibility of such a course of action is, so to speak, parenthetic. The ideal of brotherhood and the need of reconciliation would certainly favor a maintenance of old relations even after divorce is permissible. Forgiveness and reconciliation are as much the supreme needs in the family as at the altar.[1] (2) There is nothing in his teachings that would lead us to believe Jesus disapproved of the separation of a married pair for other causes than the one which would justify divorce. But remarriage on the part of either husband or wife who are thus separated would be regarded by him as a violation of the marriage union that still exists between them.

The ground for this definiteness is not difficult to discover. Marriage, both in its lower and its higher aspects, is the basis of family unity. Family life is the most sacred of all relations outside of the relation between God and man. It is not to be violated even in look and thought. Adultery may be committed even when lust never passes beyond the licentious glance.[2] In the same proportion as the natural sanctity of marriage is

[1] Matt. 5 : 23, 24.
[2] Matt. 5 : 27, 28.

injured, in the same proportion is the nature of man outraged and ideal fraternity broken. To dishonor this first of human relationships is to loosen the bonds of society, to lower present social ideals, to do injury to the essential nature of both the man and the woman. It was, therefore, not in the spirit of a purist or a fanatic that Jesus thus put checks upon divorce, but in that of the ethical and social philosopher. Nor — and this is a re-markable thing — is there a trace of the current formal conception that the husband had any prop-erty rights in his wife. On the contrary, as will presently appear, Jesus, to a surprising degree, anticipated to-day's belief in the equality of the sexes. It was this as well as the underlying principles of his ideal society that led him in the face of popular opinion thus to formulate these strict statutes. Modern sentiment, like the legis-lation and the sentiment of the professional teachers of his day, is opposed to such severity in the morals of matrimony. Marriage is assuming much more the character of a legal status than of a natural union. Its continuance is increasingly believed to be dependent upon the desires of the parties concerned and the decision of the courts. So far as the mere legal separation of unequally or ill-matched persons is concerned, the ideal described by Jesus would not antagonize this modern tendency, but the general consent of past and present moral teachers and statesmen agrees with his noble rejection of the admissibility of the scandalous travesties of life's most sacred union, to which nowadays these separations generally lead. We are not now concerned with the practicability of such an ideal; it may be too absolute for an imperfect society. But it can at least be suggested that there are grounds for hesitation before one admits that the spirit animating this part of the social teaching of Jesus has been materially surpassed by much of to-day's divorce legislation.[1]

III

It is characteristic of the balance of Jesus that at this point he introduces something in the nature of an exception to this general teaching. Although marriage is thus sacred, and although in it there is one of the nucleus points of the kingdom, yet all men are not to marry. There is something pathetic

[1] For an opposite view of the teaching of Jesus, see Tissot, *Le Mariage et le Divorce*, ch. ix., and a careful statement by Carroll D. Wright in Crafts, *Practical Christian Sociology*, 446–452. It should not be forgotten that the attempt is being made here simply to discover the exact ideal of Jesus. The question of its practicability and its gradual realization belongs to the discussion of sociological dynamics.

as well as humorous in the anxiety shown by the disciples over his stern teaching.[1] It seems to them that if divorce be thus forbidden it were better not to marry at all! Jesus, with characteristic tact, grants them their conclusion, but supplies it with premises of a much loftier standard, and in his treatment of the matter presents one of the fundamental teachings of his entire system, viz., that a good thing must always be sacrificed for a better thing. No man, unless like Origen he be utterly blinded by an ascetic and fanatic fervor, could ever misinterpret the intense words in which Jesus expresses this axiom. They simply form one of those characteristic additions with which he so often modifies a truth otherwise absolutely stated. While marriage is supremely good, yet if for any cause it stand in the way of accepting the blessings of the kingdom of heaven, it is to be avoided. The welfare of others, the advancement of the ideal society require the individual to yield private rights. Whether it be to avoid the propagation of an hereditary disease or criminal proclivity, or whether it be that some great mission in life may be the better fulfilled, celibacy may often be the only form of life a man should adopt. But the men who have thus "made themselves eunuchs for the

1 Matt. 19 : 20.

kingdom of heaven's sake"[1] are no more holier than men who have sacrificed other individual desires and goods for the common weal. The words of Jesus are a restatement of the familiar teaching of the sacrificed eye and hand.[2] And Jesus himself lived by this standard, a celibate but not an ascetic.

But possibly it may be urged that another exception may be derived from the admission by Jesus that Moses had yielded to the "hardness of heart" on the part of the Jews,[3] and had allowed divorce on such grounds as might easily be made to permit no small latitude. In the light of this recognition of an adjustment of legislation to a people's capacity, may we not have a modifying clause of the ideal legislation?

The objection is weighty, but, disregarding the advisability of admitting such an accommodation in case of reformatory legislation, as a modification of an actual ideal of family life set forth by Jesus it is not to be admitted. Jesus is here confessedly setting forth a social ideal for the present age and for the very people he addressed. By his own statements it cannot possibly apply to the perfect society of the age to come, since then divorce like marriage will be a question outgrown.

[1] Matt. 19:12.   [2] Matt. 5:29, 30.   [3] Matt. 19:8; Mark 10:5.

To admit this modification would be to destroy his social ideal of mutual fraternity. It would make him in the same breath with which he declares the indissoluble union of two persons to be the divine plan of creation, also declare that after all such a union is not essential in every case, but may be replaced by a more or less indiscriminate multiplication of partners. Such a contradiction, it must be remembered, does not confront the man who regards marriage as simply a contract which guarantees certain peculiar rights to the two consenting parties. In such a conception law makes and law can unmake the union. But with Jesus marriage is a fact, not a definition. God and nature join; man and law cannot separate. He may be a dreamer. He certainly is not inconsistent.[1]

Two further questions are, however, not answered : Would not this position of Jesus admit divorce in case the marriage were broken in its psychical side, though not on its physical; that is, in case of an utter destruction of conjugal love, although neither husband and wife had otherwise broken marital obligations ? and, second, would

[1] For a brief discussion of these two possible conceptions of marriage see Dike, "Theory of the Marriage Tie," *Andover Review*, December, 1893.

not the spirit if, indeed, not the letter of Jesus be met in case of a divorce granted for an absolute desertion; that is, would not Jesus so far favor the position of modern law as to grant that desertion is, if not constructive adultery, at least a real severing of both physical and psychical union?

So far as the first of these questions is concerned, a moment's thought will convince one that this is precisely the thing Jesus is attacking. Metaphysically, it may be, such a position would be permissible. Practically, it would be free love. And, further, it is necessary to remember that in this social teaching Jesus is not dealing with the possible situations of isolated individuals, but with society as such. He is here subject to the necessities that surround all those who provide for the common good. It is not to the point, therefore, to plead a resulting hardship in specific cases. But it is not so easy to answer the second of these two questions categorically. It is evident that desertion might easily be regarded as a redefinition of "adultery," and that it has good reasons for being admitted on the very grounds by which Jesus establishes his general position. In this case, therefore, we have a question of interpretation of legislation, and there will always be opportunity for question. But it nevertheless seems tolerably

clear that, except perhaps in extreme cases, such
redefinition is at once repugnant and dangerous.
Waiving the exceedingly important considerations
as to the ease by which such a conception of adultery
could be abused, it seems sufficient to say that as
a general interpretation this view is to be rejected.
It involves conditions too similar to those which
Jesus immediately attacked, and it is a too severe
strain upon the plain meaning of the term[1] used
by Jesus; it is hinging too many possibilities upon
an exceptive clause which is itself omitted by an
original source.

But it should again be said that we are not so
much concerned with the applications of the teaching of Jesus as with the discovery of his conception of the ideal forms of social life. It may very
likely appear that in an attempt at realizing his
ideal of social purity, legislators and reformers
must, like Moses, concede much to the hardness
of men's hearts.

IV

It follows from this noble conception of marriage that woman is placed by Jesus upon a
plane of equality with man. She is neither the
creature of his fancy, nor is she in a relation of
either real or formal subjection. Here, it is true,

[1] πορνεία.

Jesus was less out of accord with the tendencies of his time. Throughout the Roman Empire there was an appreciable advance in the position of woman. Except in the ascetic philosophy of the Essenes, among the Jews the wife had always held a relatively high position, and among the Romans this was increasingly true through the neglect of the forms of marriage involving *in manu* relations. But even after this has been said, no person acquainted with Jewish or Roman life of the first century would deny that Jesus gives woman a position essentially different from that accorded her by either philosophy or custom.

While among the Romans the steady emancipation through which woman was passing was winning the contempt of the professional moralist and the laughter of the writer of comedy; and while in Judea the noble ideal of motherhood was being lowered by the ease by which divorce might be obtained; with Jesus there is neither a recognition of a past subjection of woman, an attempt at her emancipation, nor a lament over the difficulties to be foreseen in the enforcement of his teaching in regard to marriage. He simply treats woman as an equal — equal in the matter of marriage and divorce, equal as a companion.

H

More than once is the despicable conceit of some
Pharisee or disciple rebuked by his exhibition of
unconventional sociability. They might wonder
or complain; but none the less he taught and
loved. All through the gospel story we find a
surprisingly high position accorded women. The
life of Jesus was to give them something more
than protection. It made them the companions
of men — equally privileged members of the new
human brotherhood. It was a virgin who bore the
Saviour; a woman to whom he, as a child, was
subject, and by whom, in all probability, he was
trained and educated;[1] to a woman, so far as
we have any record, he gave the first clear proclamation of his Messiahship.[2] His first miracle
was wrought because of the faith and at the
solicitation of his mother.[3] A woman, who because of her grateful faith poured over him the
costly ointment, is the only person to whom
he promised an immortality of remembrance.[4]
Women ministered to his needs and supplied
him the means of support.[5] Among the last
words Jesus spoke upon the cross were those
with which he commended Mary to the care of

[1] Luke 2 : 52. For training of children see Edersheim, *Life of
Jesus the Messiah*, and Stapfer, *Palestine in the Time of Christ*.
[2] John 4 : 7 *sq*.   [3] John 2 : 4 *sq*.   [4] Mark 14 : 9.   [5] Luke 8 : 3.

his beloved disciple.[1] A woman was the first at the tomb,[2] the first to see the risen Christ,[3] the first to believe on him, and the first to bear testimony to the resurrection.[4] And is it altogether without suggestiveness that in his words to Martha he should have carried his teaching into the heart of housewifely cares and have lifted women's life above cooking as he lifted men's above money-getting?[5]

The by no means improbable story[6] of his encounter with one unfortunate woman, which so long held a position in our canonical collection, is a natural outgrowth of the thought of a generation upon which his infinite tact and delicacy had made a profound impression. And it was but an application of his noble conception of the dignity of womanhood and wifehood when the apostles and early Christians proscribed licentiousness as a defiling of the temple of the Holy

[1] John 19 : 26, 27.

[2] Matt. 28 : 1; Mark 16 : 1; John 20 : 1.

[3] Matt. 28 : 9; John 20 : 11.   [4] John 20 : 18.

[5] Luke 10 : 38–42. It cannot have escaped notice that Luke especially among the evangelists gives prominence to the liberality of Jesus. See Plummer, *Critical and Exegetical Commentary on the Gospel according to Luke, xlii.*

[6] John 7 : 53–8 : 11. It is not, perhaps, without significance that ἀγαπάω is the word used to describe the attitude of Jesus toward women. Luke 7 : 47; John 11 : 5.

Ghost,[1] and refused to break irregular though real marriages that were found to exist among converts from heathenism at the time of their entrance into the church.[2]

And throughout the gospel story the same equality is observed. He made them members of his society with no distinctively low position, and within the early church their worth was recognized and their needs supplied as in the case of men. As he says who more than all the New Testament writers has appreciated the real significance of this phase of the work of Jesus, "In Christ there is neither male nor female."[3]

Two objections may be raised to this position : On the one hand it may be urged that he some-times spoke brusquely to women — even to his mother.[4] But this objection is trivial and would doubtless never have been raised except for the unusually awkward and harsh expression in our English version. On the other hand, it may be urged with far more force that Jesus never ex-pressly attacked those social customs that force women into infamy, or those conventionalities that have for centuries made her politically and legally the inferior of man ; in short, that he never poses

[1] 1 Cor. 6 : 15–20.   [3] Gal. 3 : 28.
[2] 1 Cor. 7 : 10, 11 ; 1 Tim. 3 : 2.   [4] John 2 : 4 ; Matt. 15 : 21–28.

as the champion of the rights of women. But neither does he expressly attack many other social sins and injustices. Nor — and time has proved this — was it needful that he should. The genus includes the species, and if once men get to incorporating the social principles he has enunciated, special forms of evil will of necessity disappear. Fortunately for the world, he who championed the cause of a repentant harlot was not the statistician of prostitution, much less its casuistical defender. He was its deadliest enemy. To demand that the friend of Mary Magdalene and the eulogist of the heathen mother and the self-sacrificing widow should preach woman suffrage; or to complain because he whose life was a continuous argument for equality and fraternity among men and women did not revise the Old Testament until it accorded with the Christian conceptions of to-day, is to ask that which is as silly as it is impossible and needless.

V

And what is true of his honoring of woman, is strikingly apparent in his regard for childhood. Jesus himself was a man without home,[1] without wife, without child; but he has left words which

[1] For this seems the most natural interpretation of Luke 9 : 57, 58, notwithstanding the proposal of Professor Bruce (*Expositor*,

have for all ages sanctified childhood.   In his own life, despite the scantiness of the records found in Luke and Matthew, there is presented an ideal of boyhood.   He rendered filial obedience to his parents and as a "child grew and waxed strong, filled with wisdom, and the grace of God was upon him." [1]   In his words over the little children who were forbidden by the disciples to come to him, he has lifted childhood into a type of character, and has given children their share in the kingdom of God.[2]   In fact, with Jesus the vocabulary of the family becomes one of choicest affection.   His disciples are his "little children," doubly dear when he is about to leave them.[3]   All earnest members of his divine brotherhood are his family.[4]

In the comparisons of Jesus we again see clearly the underlying Christian ideal of the family. Here, as in the case of women, among his words there is no exhortation to either paternal or filial love.   The apostle, less filled with a profound confidence in the inmost nature of man and more concerned with halting converts, bids sons obey their parents and fathers not to provoke their

October, 1896) to regard the words as figuratively portraying his rejection by the leaders of his fatherland.

[1] Luke 2 : 40 ; cf. Luke 2 : 52.

[2] Matt. 19 : 13–15; Mark 10 : 13–16; Luke 18 : 15–17.

[3] John 13 : 33; Mark 10 : 24.   [4] Matt. 12 : 49, 50.

children to wrath.[1] But such commands were
impossible for Jesus. With him paternal love is
as human and natural as life. To command it
would have been to make the holiest of instincts
the product of effort. From the very method of
his teaching Jesus must needs have started with
some absolute ideal to which he might compare
spiritual relations, and which, already understood,
would make intelligible that which was difficult to
understand. Other teachers have felt the same
need, and this highest type of holiest relations has
been found in many things — numerical harmo-
nies, nature, the state. Jesus found it in the family.
Even among evil men the paternal instinct gives
good gifts and the deception of a child is unthink-
able.[2] Love and kindliness between brothers are
spontaneous[3] and their absence is a type of all
that is selfish and ungodlike.[4] To give up family
relations is the supreme test of loyalty.[5] Thus it
is that, as has already appeared is his habit, Jesus
here using the noblest forms and words for his
noblest teaching, makes the members of the

[1] Eph. 6 : 1, 4; Col. 3 : 20, 21.

[2] Matt. 7 : 9–11; Luke 11 : 11–13.

[3] Matt. 5 : 47; John 8 : 42.

[4] Luke 15 : 25, 32; cf. Matt. 5 : 22; 10 : 21.

[5] Matt. 19 : 29. Here belong the severe commands of Luke 9 :
57–62.

divine society brothers; while paternal love is
his representation of the love of God,[1] and the
family as a unit, his type of that divine society
toward which humanity with a Christ within it
must move.

It is because of this supreme position of family
relations, assigned and presupposed by Jesus, that
he has no need to prescribe any minute regulations as to education and the other duties owed
to and by children.   His own day was full of
educational opportunities for boys and girls, both
Roman and Jew, but this was not the cause of
his omission of this phase of child-life.   As in the
case of the position of women, his ideal of the
family is dynamic.   Here, as in so much of his
work, the real significance of Jesus lies farthest
from that of a mere tabulator of duties.   He could
afford to leave his ideal society with its details not
filled in, because with the ideal he gave also evolu-
tionary forces.   Once possessed by the ideal of
brotherhood, and once, be it never so feebly,
under the influence of these spiritual forces, each
generation could be trusted to transform the world
in which it lived into a greater or less approxima-
tion to the kingdom.   In this disregard of the
temporary, and in his sublime trust in the salva-

[1] Luke 15 : 11–32.

bility of human society, and especially in the possibility of recuperation that lies in the health and goodness of social instincts if once they are allowed a normal spiritual environment, Jesus stands infinitely removed from even the best of his followers. They argue where he believes. They legislate where he inspires. The office of each is necessary, for the apostles, like the Christians of subsequent epochs, must needs incarnate the principles of Jesus in the midst of different social forces and thus form one stage in the successive approaches to that new society whose ideal Jesus set before humanity. But he is the architect; they are the craftsmen, the hewers of wood and stone.

VI

It is at this point that Jesus leaves the family, the first social unit. He has given no specific regulations in regard to the up-bringing of children. He has not concerned himself with those difficult domestic problems with which the apostles were to be so mightily tried. It was enough, apparently, for him to have applied clearly the supreme social ideals of divine sonship and human fraternity to this first great union of humanity. He has shown that such applications involve above all unity of the family and therefore the sanctity of the marriage tie and the dignity of woman. The carrying of such principles into the details of human relationship, with the accommodation of them to the needs and possibilities of an imperfect society, was left by Jesus especially to his immediate followers.   But his words were enough.   Through all the difficulties that such accommodation involved they kept fast hold upon the noble parallel of their Master.   As with him the new social order was to be a family with God as its father and men as its children, so with them the church was the bride of the Lamb, and every fatherhood and family in heaven and on earth was named of that great Father before whom they daily bowed the knee.

CHAPTER V

THE STATE

"THE conception of the state," says Bluntschli,[1] "has to do with the nature and essential characteristics of actual states. The idea or ideal of the state presents a picture, in the splendor of imaginary perfection, of the state as not yet realized, but to be striven for. The conception of the state can be discovered only by history; the idea of the state is called up by philosophical speculation."

No one will be apt to expect from Jesus an historical study of the conception of the state. He was a student neither of history nor of politics. But there is no lack of facts that go to prove that men since his day have looked to him as furnishing an ideal of statecraft almost as much as of morals and religion.

I

If one looks to the early Christian communities for their political attitude, one is immediately

[1] *The Theory of the State*, Eng. trans., p. 15.

struck with the prevalent policy of *laissez faire*.
It is true that the hospitable Jason[1] of Thessa-
lonica suffered at the hands of his fellow-citizens
for harboring those who were acting " contrary to
the decrees of Cæsar, saying that there is another
king, one Jesus," and it is by no means impossible
that others of the Christian community may also
have become involved.[2]   But both he and they
were the victims of a religious persecution that
sought to justify itself by the use of terms treason-
able in sound.   The attitude which the churches
ordinarily held to the Roman administration was
that seen in the anti-revolutionary advice given by
Paul to the Christians at Corinth — " Let each man
abide in that calling wherein he was called "[3] —
and in the more specific teaching of the later
epistles, to " pray for kings and all that are in
high places,"[4] and to be " subject to every ordi-
nance of man for the Lord's sake : whether it be
to the king, as supreme ; or to governors, as sent
by him for vengeance on evil-doers and for praise
to them that do well," to " fear God, honor the

---

[1] Acts 17 : 1–9.   [2] 1 Thess. 2 : 14.

[3] 1 Cor. 7 : 20. The attitude of Paul himself is seen in his appeal
to Cæsar (Acts 25 : 10) as well as in his use of his Roman citizen-
ship as a means of escaping the designs of the Jews (Acts 16 : 37;
22 : 25).

[4] 1 Tim. 2 : 2.

king." [1] This law-abiding spirit of the early Christians is further evidenced not only by similar appeals of Clement of Rome [2] and of Polycarp,[3] but also by the well-known incident reported by Pliny [4] to Trajan of their giving up their religious common meal in order not to appear guilty of breaking the imperial law against sodalities.

But by the time of Justin Martyr [5] we find the Christian expressions concerning the kingdom of God less carefully guarded, and a misconception of their teachings on the part of the heathen growing easy. Probably these misconceptions were not altogether unfounded. For it would be but natural if the persecutions through which the church passed should lead it to emphasize the coming kingdom. To Tertullian the conversion of the Cæsars seemed as unlikely as the elevation of a Christian to the imperial throne,[6] while Origen

---

[1] I Peter 2:13, 17.

[2] Epistle to Corinthians, chs. 60, 61.

[3] Epistle to Philippians, ch. 12. Other instances are given in Sanday and Headlam, *Romans*, p. 372.

[4] Pliny, *Epistles*, bk. x., ch. 97. See also Ramsay, *The Church in the Roman Empire*, ch. x. The absence of revolutionary tendencies is also evidenced by the tradition preserved by Hegesippus and Eusebius that Domitian sent to Palestine for the relatives of Jesus on the ground that they were planning a revolt, but finding them innocent peasants he sent them back.

[5] For instance, *Apology*, ii., 58.   [6] *Apology*, ch. 21.

replies to the sneer of Celsus that Christians had best undertake the management of the state, "In whatever city we are, we have another country, which is founded by the word of God."[1]   From this time on the more ascetic bodies of Christians seem to have withdrawn themselves as far as possible from civil duties, while the more moderate party was content to endure the state as a necessary evil.

The new significance in the empire given the church by Constantine and his successors placed the political import of Christianity in an entirely new light.   On the one hand the Christians saw the triumph of Christ in their unexampled political power, while on the other, especially in the West where the misery of the fifth century began to be felt, pagan writers charged the misfortunes of the time to the new Christian rulers.   In meeting this charge, Augustine rightly enough emphasizes the evil political tendencies to be seen under the heathen emperors, but in the *De Civitate Dei* also defends Christian teaching from the charge of being inimical to the state.   "Let them give us," he urges, "such warriors as the Christian doctrines require they should be ; . . . such subjects ; . . .

[1] See Neander, *History of the Christian Religion and Church*, I., 272.

such kings and judges; such payers and receivers
of tribute as they ought to be according to the
Christian doctrine; and would they still venture
to assert that this doctrine is opposed to the state?
Nay, would they not rather confess without hesitation, that, if it were followed, it would prove the
salvation of the state." Yet Augustine does not
attempt to construct any theory of the state from
scriptural data. He distinctly turns away [1] from
such an endeavor. The City of God is not an ideal
commonwealth, but a heavenly, an eschatological
reign of peace which is to be expected, but not
enjoyed in this age. Priests and prophets had
foretold it, the saints of Israel had prayed to see
it; the sacred books were full of its ceaseless conflict with its evil counterpart, that fruit of Adam's
fall, the earthly state. And before this glorious
millennial age could come, this enemy must forever disappear.

With the revival of the Roman Empire by
Charlemagne, and especially with the later attempts at a dual empire during the Middle Ages,
the theoretical side of politics became increasingly
dependent upon scriptural supports. It was characteristic of the exegetical processes of the time
that such support should often be gained by a sort

[1] *De Civitate Dei*, bk. 19, ch. 17.

of allegorizing process from expressions utterly lacking in political content. Not to plunge into the mysteries of Daniel and the Apocalypse, nothing is more fundamental in the argument one meets constantly in mediæval documents concerned with the bitter struggle between pope and emperor, than the appeal to the two swords.[1] It is impossible to discover who for the first time used this remarkable argument to establish the need of a spiritual and temporal head for the state. By the time it is used by the first combatants of the eleventh and twelfth centuries, it has acquired universal assent as inspired teaching, and the only matter of concern is whether both swords were given to Peter, thus proving the superiority of the pope ; or one each to Peter and John, thus establishing the coördinate power of the emperor. By the time of the formularies found in the Sachsenspiegel, so far as the Holy Roman Empire is concerned, it has become the epitome of mediæval political theory. It is not to our purpose to notice the extraordinary logic of the vigorous letter of Henry IV. which accompanied the equally vigor-

[1] Luke 22 : 38. And they said, Lord, behold here are two swords. And he said unto them, It is enough. Boniface VIII. and the Bull *Unam Sanctam* show the possibility of this sort of reasoning.

ous letter of the German bishops to Gregory VII.,[1] but it cannot be overlooked that not only does Henry appeal to the words of Peter[2] and Paul,[3] but that he also expressly states that the royal authority, like the papal, is the gift of Jesus Christ. Frederick Barbarossa argues quite as directly and forcibly.[4] On the other hand, the popes established their claims to superiority by the "plurality of the keys."[5]

These are by no means all the texts used by the mediæval writers and combatants. As Bryce says, "Every passage was seized upon when submission to the powers that be is enjoined, every instance cited where obedience had actually been rendered to imperial officials, a special emphasis being laid on the sanction which Christ himself had given to Roman dominion by pacifying the world through Augustus by being born at the time of the taxing,

[1] *Monumenta Germaniæ Historica*, Leges II., 44 *sq.*

[2] I Pet. 2: 17.

[3] Gal. I : 8.

[4] For instance, in his remarkable proclamation following the affair at Besançon: "Cumque per electionem principum a solo Deo regnum et imperium nostrum sit, qui in passione Christi filii sui duobus gladiis necessariis regendum orbem subjecit, cumque Petrus apostolus hac doctrina mundum informaverit: 'Deum timete, regem honorificate,'" etc. Bluntschli reprints (*Theory of the State*, p. 40 n.) the sentence from the *Sachsenspiegel* mentioned above.

[5] Matt. 16: 19.

I

by paying tribute to Cæsar, by saying to Pilate, 'Thou couldest have no power at all against me except it were given thee from above.'"[1] It is not too much to say that mediæval political theory is one branch of the all-embracing theology of the times. Not merely within the circle of imperial ideas, but generally, "the state was held to be an organization willed and created by God."[2] Thus Thomas Aquinas, although he does not greatly appeal to Scripture, regards the political state not as did Augustine as a consequence of the fall, but as a necessary part of the world's life. Law in his estimation was an outflowing of the divine nature.

But the attempt to discover a divine and scriptural basis for the state has been by no means limited to the Middle Ages. There have always been Savonarolas who would make Christ king in their cities, and Cromwells who would establish a kingdom of saints. Throughout the fierce struggles that gave birth to modern Europe and erected in America the United States, armies have repeatedly alternated drill with prayer and fighting with catechising. One has but to recall such careers as

[1] *Holy Roman Empire*, p. 113. Dante (*De Monarchia*) is probably the best representative of this mediæval political theology from the side of the empire.

[2] Bluntschli, p. 57.

those of Calvin and Zwingli, William of Orange and Winthrop; such extravagances as those at Münster; such reigns as that of James II. of England; such hereditary hatreds as that between the north and south of Ireland; such legislation as that of Massachusetts Bay, to feel at once that politics have always been profoundly affected by theologies.

But after all, few if any of the theologico-political thinkers of the past have troubled to separate the teaching of Jesus from the general teaching of both Old and New Testaments. It may very well be that in this failure to distinguish, not only between the history of the Jews and the teachings of Christianity, but also between the teaching of Jesus and that of the apostles, men have lost some of the distinction that appears between the aims of Jesus and those of the apostles, as well as between his ideal and their more or less incomplete attempts at realizing such an ideal.

II

Jesus nowhere gives systematic teaching in regard to politics. His attitude towards the state and political relations is to be seen, if at all, in his own life, in scattered statements, and in general comparisons and implications.

As regards his own life, it is very evident
that he obeyed the local and imperial governments under which he lived, and that he distinctly refused to be made a governor or a king,
or in any way to be involved in political revolution, preferring death to political agitation.[1]
While it is, of course, in the main true that
this attitude of conformity was due to the conditions which governed his work as a religious
teacher, it is none the less probable that in it
there was a recognition of the necessity and the
rightful claims of the state.

The principles which he enunciates are very
general and scattered.   Nowhere have we anything like the fulness and the explicitness that
mark his teachings in regard to marriage and
divorce.   The most celebrated text,[2] "Render
unto Cæsar the things that are Cæsar's, and
unto God the things that are God's," is rather
an avoidance of specific teaching than an enunciation of a principle.   The position in which
Jesus found himself precluded any unequivocal
answer.[3]   That was why his opponents asked

[1] John 6: 15; 18: 36; Acts 1: 5 *sq.*
[2] Matt. 22: 18–22.
[3] The taxes were a constant cause of revolt.   See Josephus, *Antiquities of the Jews*, 18: 1: 1–6; 20: 5: 2; Acts 5: 37.

the question. His answer, therefore, was one
that might be interpreted either favorably or
unfavorably according to the conception his opponents held as to whether or not Cæsar really
owned the coins.   Once grant (as the account
would lead us to suppose they did grant) that
"the image and superscription" on the coin
implied the sovereignty of Cæsar, and the reply
of Jesus would of necessity pronounce the payment of taxes legitimate.[1]   Deny that implication and his reply says nothing of the law. It
is, therefore, obvious that any wide application
of this text to the exigencies of politics must
first of all presuppose the sovereign rights of
the ruler.   Besides, it is clear that in the mind
of Jesus the emphasis was upon the thought of
rendering to God the things that were his.
The entire reply was a rebuke to their insidious
quibbling.

If, however, Jesus be credited with something
more than an *ad hominem* argument, it is possible to go a step farther and discover in these
words something like a genuine political prin-

[1] That the effigy was regarded by the Jews as implying sovereignty is clear from the fact in the revolt against Hadrian they re-
stamped the Roman coins.   See Madden, *Coins of the Jews*, 176, 203,
and Renan, *Life of Jesus* (Am. ed., 1895), 337 n.

ciple. The Jews by using the coins — for we
dismiss as trifling the question as to whether
such coins were actually in existence — in so far
were served by the Roman government. They,
therefore, owed it some service in return. This
service was the payment of taxes. But it will
not do to press this, and it is much safer to say
that in these words Jesus lays down no principle as to the righteousness or unrighteousness
of any form of government than to plead them
either as an excuse for submission to tyranny or
as an incentive to a struggle for independence.

Hardly more direct is their application to the
relations of church and state. Despite the use
made of them to lay "the foundation of spiritual as distinct from temporal power, thus making firm the base of true liberalism and true
civilization,"[1] it is self-evident that Jesus was
not arguing in regard to a state church or any
kindred subject, but was calling his questioners
back to a sense of their duties to God. In the
light of what has been said it seems by no
means clear that Jesus would exclude obedience
to law from the duties of a religious man.

In Matthew 17:27 we have another instance
in which he apparently submitted to the de-

[1] Renan, *Life of Jesus* (Am. ed., 1895), 338.

mands of the tax collector and even justified it
by the aid of a miracle. But even if one were
not to reject the entire account on the ground
that the miraculous element contained is inhar-
monious with the other miraculous elements of
the New Testament, it would by no means follow that even in this text we have data for political teaching. The tax which he so paid was
not a political tax, but a religious levy for the
support of the temple at Jerusalem.[1] It is still
true that Jesus submitted to an existing authority, albeit ecclesiastical rather than political,
although not altogether without certain protests.
At any rate, the illustration would far better
serve as an argument for tithes than for taxes.
But the whole incident reads quite as much as
anything else like a rebuke for the over-zealous
haste with which Peter promised to pay the
temple tax. It is a most astonishing exegesis
that finds in it an argument for freeing the
clergy from taxation!

More distinct is the answer given by Jesus to
the well-meant boast of Pilate[2] that he had the
power of punishing or acquitting: "Thou wouldst

---

[1] Edersheim, *Life and Times of Jesus the Messiah*, II., 111-113.
See also Exodus 30: 11 *sq.*; Neh. 10: 32 *sq.* The Mishna has a
separate treatise on the subject.   [2] John 19: 11.

have no authority against me, except it were given thee from above." At the first glance it would appear as if these words are to be taken according to their historical interpretation and thus commit Jesus to the theory of the divine right of kings, not to mention the whole mass of pusillanimity and casuistry known as the doctrine of Passive Obedience. But it seems somewhat strange to think of Jesus at this supreme hour setting forth a political theory. It is much more natural to regard these words as a part of his philosophy of providence.[1] They do indeed justify Pilate as a judge, and express submission to a government as to any fact of society, but they by no means make the right of kings any more divine than a myriad other rights. The song of Pippa,

> "God's in his heaven,
> All's right with the world,"

would come far nearer expressing the attitude of Jesus than the sermons of Bishop Berkeley.

Nor when we pass from the search for definite statements to a consideration of the implications and the comparisons of the teachings of Jesus do we gain any more definite results. He frequently

[1] Compare Matt. 6: 25–34.

uses certain phases of royal life to illustrate his teachings : the kingdom of God in some respects he said was like a would-be king who had rebellious subjects ;[1] or a king who gave a marriage supper to his son, only to find himself insulted ;[2] or a king who was more merciful than one of his subjects ;[3] while the misfortunes that come upon a kingdom torn by civil war, furnished him arguments for proving his own innocence of complicity with Satan.[4] These comparisons, coupled with the absence of any serious[5] criticism of royalty, make it safe to say, that while we are lacking in definite political teaching emanating from Jesus, we cannot maintain to the contrary, that he regarded government as an evil. But his kingdom was indeed not of this world,[6] and these comparisons yield no data for generalization.

In the light of these facts it is certainly a strange use of language to speak of the words

---

[1] Luke 19 : 11 *sq.*
[2] Matt. 22 : 2.
[3] Matt. 18 : 23 *sq.*
[4] Mark 3 : 24; Matt. 12 : 25 *sq.*
[5] For no one except a fanatic would see in the somewhat cutting reference to the luxury of courts (Matt. 11 : 8; Luke 7 : 25) anything opposed to monarchy as such. Nor do the references to trials before kings and judges (Matt. 10 : 18) imply any opposition to the institutions they represent.
[6] John 18 : 36.

of Jesus as those of a teacher of politics, and
the Sermon on the Mount as a political document.[1]
It is true that the teachings there contained, if
once carried out, will, as Augustine protested,
produce good men and, therefore, in so far, good
citizens. And it is by no means difficult so to
use language as to make Jesus one of the long
line of victims upon the altar of political reform.
Was not the treasurer of his little society of a
dozen men a type of the "boodler" who, having
made what he could from the proposed kingdom,
sold out its king? And did not Jesus himself
perish as a revolutionist — a king of the Jews?
But, after all, such a view is a tribute to its pro-
pounder's homiletical ingenuity rather than to his
understanding of the real life and significance
of Jesus. If he were indeed essentially a political
reformer or idealist, is it not an astonishing thing
that he should have left no more teachings in
regard to the state than these scattered, and on

[1] So, if we can understand his position, Herron, *The Christian
Society*, p. 51. "It [The Sermon on the Mount] is in no sense a
sermon, least of all a discourse on individual piety, but a political
document, given on a political occasion, as truly as the Great
Charter or the Declaration of Independence." But it is possible
that the author does not expect these words to be taken literally,
but rather as impassioned rhetoric to express the fact that the
teachings of Jesus have a bearing upon political questions.

the whole, obscure texts? Even the apostles gave more political teaching than he.

III

Was Jesus then an anarchist?

The question is absurd if one means by anarchy the philosophy of dynamite and terror. But this, of course, is only a caricature of a far more tenable political philosophy. Proudhon's "anarchic government" was to be no more full of violence than the "natural" state of Rousseau. The name has unfortunate associations, but, at least as the name of a philosophy, may stand for an ideal condition, which is to be the expression of law. But this law is no longer as with Thomas Aquinas the outflow of the divine nature, but is rather the expression of a human nature that is instinctively to do that which is good not only in the eyes of its possessor, but also in those of his neighbors.

"Anarchy is not inconsistent with association, but only with enforced association. It means simply a state of society in which no one is bound or obliged to do anything (whether to associate with others or anything else); it is not opposed to order, but only to enforced order; nor to rule, but only to obligatory rule. In other words it is synonymous with liberty. Under such a system, individuals would simply be left free to do as they chose; compulsion would disappear; the only bonds in society would be moral bonds."[1]

There could be no inherent objection to calling Jesus this sort of anarchist if his teachings were sufficiently distinct to justify the use of any political term.   It might, indeed, by its sensational connections attract new attention to his words.   It would not be the first time novelty has done yeoman service as truth.   And it must be admitted that at first glance there is something of similarity between Jesus' conception of his new social order and this benign and harmless political metaphysics, which, like a sheep in wolf's clothing, is doing its best by masquerading under an ill-omened name to startle the world into believing it of practical importance.   But unless our conception of the teaching of Jesus is altogether incorrect, not only would it be ill-advised to use the term anarchy in speaking of his teaching, but

[1] Salter, *Anarchy or Government*, p. 7.   Two other opinions may be requoted from this little work : " In heaven nothing like what we call government on earth can exist." — Channing, *Works*, p. 361.   " Strict anarchy may be the highest conceivable grade of perfection of social existence ; but, if all men spontaneously did justice and loved mercy, it is plain that all swords might advantageously be turned into ploughshares, and that the occupation of judges and police would be gone." — Huxley, *Essays*, I., 39.

it would commit him to notions of government and society, which, if we may judge from his words, were utterly absent from his thought. For instance, much of the plausibility of this irenic anarchy depends upon the conception of the state as a mere coercive regulator of individuals who need an umpire to decide and enforce the extent to which each must yield to the other in the interest of social peace. Once conceive of the state as something more than this agent of coercion, and the most captivating argument of the anarchist weakens before some utopia of the socialist pure and simple. Now the words of Jesus should not be forced to train with those of either school. His thought is not political. He stands no more committed to an idea of government as a keeper of the peace than to the idea of government as a sort of executive committee of a democracy. We may say that in certain particulars his teaching would agree with either conception. But the point of its agreement is not within the sphere of speculative or practical politics, but within that of individual duties and social regeneration. One can no more call him an anarchist because he gives no political teaching than he can call him a surgeon because he never speaks of medicines.

And, indeed, his silence in itself is opposed to all anti-governmental opinions. For it is not of the same sort as his silence with regard to social infamies. In such cases as slavery and prostitution, his silence was possible because in his general teachings are contained forces which would inevitably bring about their destruction. But, in the case of government, it is by no means true that the fundamental principles of his ideal social order are destructive. If we once more look at the matter historically, it becomes evident that in the interpretation of his own age his silence was not regarded as anarchistic; and in later times it has been true that while some peoples who have come under his direct influence have developed democracies, in no case of importance, at least, is it true that they have been hostile to governments as such. The Puritan was no less a champion of strong government than the Cavalier. The contrary interpretation which has been placed upon his teachings by some Christians of different centuries was clearly sporadic and due to a misapprehension of the kingdom of God. That the Christians of the early centuries regarded their faith as inimical to the Roman Empire may be true, but even in this case, in a singularly materialistic fashion, they expected that in the place of that empire which was persecuting them, or which was going down before the barbarians because of its vice, there would come, not anarchy, but another kingdom which would be genuinely monarchical — the everlasting kingdom of their Christ. In other words, the very misconception of the Christians of the third and fourth centuries of the teachings of Jesus in regard to the kingdom is an evidence that they did not regard these teachings as anarchistic.

And, indeed, the whole philosophy of Christ in regard to man, both real and ideal, points to the same conclusion. The union which he holds up is not that of an aggregation, but is organic. The kingdom of God is the union of brothers over whom God himself is to reign. Mankind is not composed of insulated individuals, but of social beings, who seek not a convenient association for exchange and other economic purposes, but an absorbing and organic union with one another as members of a family. If Jesus forbids his disciples to be called rabbi,[1] it is not only that he may teach them a lesson of humility and equality, but also because he himself is their Master. Indeed, within the little group of his immediate followers there is a hint of there having been some organiza-

[1] Matt. 23 : 8.

tion.[1] To imagine that Jesus was so visionary as
to fancy that the unregulated promptings of a
community are sufficient to insure order, is to
forget his feeding of the five thousand,[2] his regard
for the conventionalities of ceremonial purifica-
tions;[3] his unwillingness to interfere with the
work of John;[4] his systematic evangelization of
Palestine;[5] the repeated counsel and instruction
which he showered upon his followers. These
facts, it is true, do not point towards a theory of
the state, but they certainly suggest a mind that
was eminently ordered and respectful of formal
rather than instinctive order.

IV

Was then Jesus a socialist, a monarchist, a democrat? Again must it be said he was neither. He
stands committed to no political teaching. In this
particular he is unique among the great teachers
who have affected the West. Others, like Plato

[1] This may be conjectured from the arrangement of the names
in the lists of the apostles (Matt. 10: 2–4; Mark 3: 16–19; Luke
6: 14–16). In all accounts the same names (so far as they can be
identified) occur in the same group of four, and the first of each of
these groups is always Peter, Philip, James.

[2] Mark 6: 14.   [3] Mark 1: 44.   [4] John 4: 1–3.

[5] Mark 1 : 35–37. Compare his sending out of his disciples for
the same purpose.

and Mahomet, have yielded to the temptation of
systematic thought or circumstances, and have
weighted their philosophy and their religion with
political teachings that were either so ideal as to
be impracticable or so practicable as to be soon outgrown. Jesus felt the force of the same temptation.[1] It was not through apathy that he refused
to enter the sphere of political thought. The
people demanded it, the professional teachers expected it, the Romans finally punished him for
it. But with that concentration and foresight that
continually grows upon the student of his life, he
held himself sternly to the duties of a preacher of
religion and life. It was enough when he had
shown the fatherly monarchy of God, and the
fraternal obedience of men. As in the case of the
family, the details through which this conception
of society should be realized would be determined
by the spirit of brotherliness and the exigencies of
circumstance and time.

If men desire the sanction of Jesus for any form
of government, they must appeal not to specific
sayings, but to this spirit which is the basis of
the ideal order. The test of a theory or a fact
of government must not be Does Jesus teach it?
but Does it make for that fraternity that is his

[1] Matt. 4 : 8.

K

ideal for society? Such a tendency is conceivably the result of almost any form of political organization. Jesus himself most naturally used the monarchical vocabulary of his people just as Plato used that of the Athenian aristocratic democracy. But he thereby stands not at all committed to monarchy as the ultimate form of government. Yet for that reason the democrat and the socialist cannot claim his exclusive authority. For it cannot be too strongly reiterated that Jesus was not a political thinker, and that he has left no divinely sanctioned form for political association. A government is Christian, not because it is of this or that form, but because it is attempting to realize the principles of fraternity and love that underlie the entire social teachings of Jesus. If it be objected that no such government can exist, that force and not love is still the essential element of the state, the only rational reply is one of doubt that is itself hope. For it may well be doubted whether the teachings of Jesus are not more operative in politics than men think; and it may well be hoped so long as this possibility lasts, that, as the conceptions of man and society and the family have more and more come under the sway of the thought of Jesus, so too politics are approaching, be it

never so slowly, that justice and altruism which
are to be the world's when once its kingdoms
have become the kingdom of the Lord and his
Christ.

And one dares hope thus in the face of Euro-
pean diplomacy and American municipalities!

CHAPTER VI

WEALTH

IF ever sanity is needed, it is in economic discussion. From the time when the Roman plebs marched back from the Sacred Mount, agitation and indignant pleas for justice have won their victories through strikes or revolution, but only when men have refused to admit the decisions of those who were able to see the issue in its proper perspective. When some strong, honest man has appeared in whom both warring parties trusted, his foresight has repeatedly averted strife and reëstablished industrial peace. And so it has come about that not the agitator but the arbitrator has been the real conserver of economic progress. But the weight as well as the need of sane judgment is doubled when the religious leader of a community undertakes the amelioration of economic distress. Too often, it must be confessed, the sympathies of a dominant religious order have been with the

wealthy or the feudal class. Too seldom has
the plea of the curate been heard in the convo-
cation of the bishops. But when decision has
fallen to those religious workers most closely in
contact with the people, then, as when the curates
of the States-General dealt the death-blow to the
first and second estates of France, traditional
privilege has given away before a new public
opinion.

I

Perhaps it is with an intuition of this fact that
so often of late men have looked to Jesus as a
possible source of industrial peace. It is not
difficult to discover an incipient reaction against
a purely materialistic sociology, and a beginning
of the enunciation of teachings, which, whether
their propounders are aware of it or not, are in
many respects similar to his. It is no longer
merely in the interests of a sanctified rhetoric
that his name is so often used, for men who
are bitterly hostile to the church and to the
Christ of the church are respectful towards the
Carpenter of Nazareth.

It would indeed be strange if one who attempted to establish a regenerate social order
should have overlooked those ambitions and strivings that make up so much of human life. We

should expect, too, that Jesus, if for no other reason than completeness of thought, would not merely give, but, as in the case of marriage, would apply his general principles. It would be, of course, unreasonable to expect him to legislate specifically for every new combination in the kaleidoscope of economic history. An itinerant preacher in Judea could hardly be expected to know of the great trade combinations of Alexandria and Rome, to say nothing of those economic changes through which the centuries were to pass. Even supposing that he had been able to foresee thus minutely the future, had Jesus attempted after the rabbinical fashion to draw up minute rules for the conduct of industrial life, he must needs have filled his brief career with toil that would have been as superfluous as incomplete. It is characteristic of genius to distinguish between the accident and the essential in human experience. Judged by the same standard Jesus is the consummate genius, for there is no phase of generic human life with which he has not sympathy and to which his great principle of fraternity does not reach.

Thus inevitably Jesus touched upon economics. Not, indeed, as the man who collects material and discovers its laws : far less as those who, after

the fashion of the schoolman, struggle with definitions in which there is neither hope nor reality;
nor yet as those prophetic hearts imagine who
see in his words panaceas of their own uncon-
scious devising; but as the economic philosopher
who seeks properly to relate all economic desires
and efforts to those other desires and strivings
which together constitute life. On no subject
does he speak oftener or with more emphasis.
Indeed, in so startling a form did he sometimes
throw his teachings that men instinctively have
refused to carry their letter into life, and when
occasionally some zealous soul has thought that
duty lay in literally following such teaching, the
courts have entrusted him to a guardian.

For this, if for no other reason, men have
slighted this phase of the teachings of Jesus,
daring to trust him as a saviour from a hell of
which he seldom spoke, but judging him incom-
petent to establish upon earth that reign of love
which was the chief object of his thought. The
Jews erected monuments to the prophets their
fathers killed: Christians in worshipping the Son
of God have done despite to the Founder of
the Kingdom.

II

Misinterpretation is here easy.   In many of his
sayings Jesus discriminates harshly against the
rich.   To the rich, to the well-fed, to the merry, is
foretold woe.[1]   "It is easier," he once said, after
he had seen an earnest, rich young man turn from
him, "for a camel to go through a needle's eye
than for a rich man to enter into the kingdom of
heaven."[2]   In the most awful of his parables he
portrays the beggar Lazarus as sharing in the joys
of the blessed, unable to carry the least of his
comforts to the rich man suffering torments across
the great gulf.[3]   Our one monument of the earliest
Christianity is full of this severity.[4]   It seems but
the corollary of this discrimination when Jesus
called upon his disciples to share their wealth with
the poor.   Such of them as had property were
bidden to sell it and to give alms,[5] and no one who
asked for aid was to be denied.   The young man
who had lived an exemplary life from his youth
was told that if he would be perfect he should sell

---

[1] Luke 6 : 24.   There is a critical possibility that these words are
not those of Jesus himself, but it is supported by argument so purely
subjective as to render conviction difficult.

[2] Matt. 18 : 24.   [4] James 1 : 10, 11; 2 : 1-7; 4 : 13; 5 : 1-6.
[3] Luke 16 : 19-31.   [5] Luke 12 : 33.

what he had and give to the poor.[1]   Nay, even if
one had his goods taken from him he was not to
seek them again.[2]   And charity was not only to
be extended, it was to be enjoyed.   When Jesus
first sent out the Twelve and (according to Luke)
subsequently the Seventy, among other directions
he gave them was to take no money and to accept
hospitality from all whom they deemed worthy.[3]
Within the immediate circle of his friends the
same principle to some extent held good, for not
only did Jesus apparently give to the poor,[4] but he
himself was supported, at least in part, by devoted
women.[5]   For Jesus was a poor man without home
of his own,[6] and dependent upon others not only
for support but for that hospitality which his own
kinsmen seemed to have refused or so to have
offered as to have made its acceptance a confession
of insanity.[7]

From one of these cases it would seem as if the
renunciation of wealth was one of the conditions of
joining the new society.   But it is not without parallels.   The fishers of the lake were called to leave
a prosperous business to become fishers of men.[8]

[1] Matt. 19 : 16–22.
[2] Matt. 5 : 42.
[3] Luke 10 : 5–7.
[4] John 13 : 29.
[5] Luke 8 : 3.
[6] Matt. 8 : 19, 20; Luke 9 : 57, 58.
[7] Mark 3 : 21.
[8] Mark 1 : 16, 17; Matt. 4 : 18, 19.

Matthew left his *octroi* station near Capernaum[1]
to follow Jesus, and even the money-changers of
the Temple saw their tables overturned and their
fellow monopolists fleeing before the Galilean who
had found his Father's house made into a den of
thieves.[2]

It would not be at all strange, therefore, if from
these teachings and facts men should have con-
cluded that the pursuit of wealth was unchristian
and wealth itself an evil rather than a good. And
so men have thought in all times since the days of
Jesus. The preaching of the church against
wealth has been equalled only by its zeal to obtain
it. Those early ascetics who saw in the body only
evil, and who sought with Simon of the Pillar to
please God by the hideous mortification of the
flesh, have been far outnumbered by the multitude
of men who have by vows of poverty as well as
celibacy endeavored to make themselves accept-
able in the eyes of God. Few have so far imitated
St. Francis as to strip off wealth and clothes alike
and start at the new birth as naked as the new
babe, but every religious revival of the Middle
Ages blossomed into fresh devotions of wealth to
order or church and of life to the sanctifying pro-

[1] Matt. 8: 9.
[2] Mark 11: 17; Matt. 21: 17; Luke 19: 46.

cesses of want.   Through the centuries in which
the leaven of Jesus has been working in society,
wealth has enormously increased, but the processes of distribution have not developed so rap-
idly as those of production.   The poor have been
always present, and the Christian church has
always endeavored, with more or less wisdom, to
do them good.[1]   They are God's poor.   But too
seldom has such benefaction perfectly understood
Jesus, and too often has it hindered the realization
of his more fundamental principles.   While Jesus
sought not the amelioration but the regeneration
of individual and society, charity has for centuries
been too often the palliative of sin and the dead-
ener of conscience.   If patriotism has been once
the last refuge of a scoundrel, charity has been a
thousand times the hypocrite's price of heaven.

Even when men have not thought there was
any special merit to be acquired by the giving
away of money, they have frequently believed
that in some way Jesus discountenanced the search
for wealth.   A conviction in the absolute authority of each unrelated word of Scripture has of
necessity plunged many earnest souls into profound difficulties.   Tolstoi, finding in the words,

[1] See, for instance, Uhlhorn, *Christian Charity in the Early Church.*

"Resist not evil," the key to Christianity, ceased to be judge and soldier.[1] Few men have been equally honest in following that which they have professed to believe the only rule of life. These words of Jesus concerning wealth have been regarded as those of a visionary, and, instead of searching for their real significance, men have been too frequently ready to class them with sayings which deal with conditions that are so far from those of the world in which we live as to belong rather to a Utopia, a land of nowhere.

III

We should expect a thinker like Jesus to say something more. Can he mean to teach that the new brotherliness is to be asceticism? Are members of the new social order to live as parasites upon an evil world? Is the normal man to be an idler and the child of God a beggar? Such we must say is the only outcome of these passages if they exhaust the teachings of Jesus.

It can hardly be replied that Jesus did not mean to lay down any principles as regards wealth. His refusal to divide an inheritance between two litigious brothers[2] was no more an act of caution than a rebuke to covetousness, and the request

---

[1] *My Religion*, Chs. i.–iii.   [2] Luke 12:13-15.

itself shows how he was regarded by those who
made it.[1]   The very fact that Luke has preserved
for us [2] so much of this sort of material that Mat-

[1] It may also have been that this request was made of Jesus
simply as a rabbi, for it was customary for rabbis to decide knotty
questions of all sorts, including those about property.   But the
Jewish laws of inheritance were so precise that there could have
been no question of " division " except one brother wanted to get
something in addition to his share.   The warning against covetousness that follows this incident is accordingly quite to the point.
Such questions would more naturally come before the authorities of
the village.   See Edersheim, *Life and Times of Jesus the Messiah*,
II., 243; Stapfer, *Palestine in the Time of Christ*, 104–5.

[2] It is evident that within the synoptic gospels there is a decided
preponderance of the teachings in regard to wealth to be found in
Luke.   A comparison of the third gospel with the other two will
discover that much of this social teaching is found in those portions
which are peculiar to Luke himself.   If we adopt the most probable view as to the common material of the gospels and make it
dependent upon two great sources, the *narrative* and the *logia*, it
must be admitted that in the former there is practically nothing
which looks like any special interest in questions concerning wealth
on the part of Jesus, and in the latter little that cannot be easily
interpreted from another point of view.   But when we come to
those peculiarities which mark the gospel according to Luke, it
becomes at once evident that we are dealing with an entirely new
spirit.   The writer of the third gospel, who was also undoubtedly
the writer of the Acts, shows himself intensely sympathetic with
the poor.   He alone has preserved for us the fact that the mother
of Jesus was a poor woman ; and that his father was a carpenter.
Alone of all the synoptists he never speaks of Jesus' having followed
a trade, and mentions that during his public ministry he was dependent upon charity for his support.   And all through his teachings we find him more than ready to show the interest of Jesus in

thew has omitted shows that the original sources
whence both derived their gospels abounded with
such teachings.   Whatever difficulty there may be
in understanding the economic teaching of Jesus
arises not from its scarcity but from its abundance.
The distorted applications which have been made
of his words have been due generally to an incomplete collection of the data to be found in the
gospels.   His view of wealth is not to be found in
this or that particular saying, but in the entire
scope and course of his life and teachings.   We

publicans and poor people, and to preserve for us those words of
denunciation of the rich or encouragement of the poor which have
made Jesus the friend of the lowly of all ages. (Thus 1 : 46–55 ;
2 : 7, 16 ; 2 : 23, 24 ; 6 : 21–25; 12 : 13–33 ; 14 : 21 ; 16 : 14 *sq.*)
It is this personal equation of Luke as well as the fact that his gospel generally gives evidence of having been composed later than
that of Matthew, that leads to the not very secure conclusion that
in 6 : 21 he has preserved a less original form of the saying of Jesus
found also in Matt. 5 : 3.   It has therefore been omitted in this discussion.   But even if the contrary view be held it should be noted that
the thought of the passage in Matthew is undoubtedly the sense of the
statement in Luke.   The poor in money are very likely to be poor in
spirit.   It should be also noticed that the words of Luke were addressed directly to the disciples.   For this reason it seems altogether
probable that if they are the original words of Jesus, they are in a
sense parabolic, like those addressed to the hungry.   Plummer,
(*Critical and Exegetical Commentary on the Gospel according to
Luke.* Introduction, xxv), in showing the impossibility of discov-
ering Ebionism in Luke, says truly " Throughout the Third Gospel
there is a protest against worldliness, but there is no protest against
wealth."

do for Jesus simply what we do for every teacher
whose method was like his, if we attempt the
discovery of a principle which underlies and a
philosophy that binds together all special teachings. In the light of this principle and philosophy
the hierarchy of special teachings may be properly
established, and the significance of scattered sayings more correctly apprehended.

In the teaching of Jesus we discover above
all his recognition of the relativity of goods.
" No servant can serve two masters." [1] His effort
is to induce men to accept not that which is
good, but that which is best. Whenever the
good comes in conflict with the better and the
best, even if it be a hand or an eye or a foot, it
must immediately be abandoned.[2] Now so far
as the individual is concerned, his highest good
consists in making his life a part of other lives.
For both manward and Godward a man is essentially a social being, and his life is imperfect in
the same proportion as it is not in union with
the life of others. Thus, even on the purely
physical side, Jesus viewed the unmarried man
as so far an incomplete man. But the hermit
is likewise an abnormal man. Jesus' ideal for
humanity is that of a divine family, and in so

[1] Matt. 6: 22–24. [2] Matt. 18: 8, 9.

far as any thing or custom renders a realization
of that ideal more difficult, in the same proportion is that something to be sacrificed. In the
light of this general principle does he examine
and pronounce upon all those social questions
with which his teachings are concerned. His
question is always not "Is this thing good in
itself?" but "Does it make toward the realization of the divine brotherhood?" Thus he
looked at marriage and said that some men for
the sake of the kingdom of heaven would remain
celibate. Thus he looked at wealth. For, like
marriage, wealth concerns not the individual
alone but society as well.

IV

Wealth must be used for the establishment of
that ideal social order whose life is that of
brothers — the kingdom of God. This is the
only possible interpretation which can be placed
upon that otherwise extraordinary parable of the
unjust steward.[1] As he by trickiness, not to say
dishonesty, had won for himself friends, so is it
possible in a nobler way for men so to use wealth
as to bind others closer to themselves. This is
one of the tests of character, this making of

[1] Luke 16 : 1–13.

friends by money. For if a man be unfaithful
in the affairs of business, Jesus regards him as
liable to be unfaithful in matters of greater importance.[1] The rich man suffering in torments
had a thought of his brothers too late, and his
wealth had made no friends. He had served
mammon, but not God. So, too, Jesus condemned[2] the rich fool who, after he had accumulated wealth, planned to use it selfishly for
his own enjoyment. In the genuine epicurean
call to his soul, "Thou hast much goods laid up
for thyself; eat, drink, and be merry," this man
published his determination to avoid all the
possibilities of benefiting society wealth put in
his hands. Wealth is therefore a desirable good
only so far as it is a means to a man's highest
development — that is, only so long as it renders him more capable of fulfilling Jesus' ideal
of fraternity. For as Jesus pertinently asked,[3]
"What shall it profit a man if he gain the whole
world and yet lose himself?" A man's heart will
be with his treasure, and there is more lasting
wealth than silver and gold.[4]

[1] Luke 16: 10, 12. Clement of Alexandria, in his little tract *The
Salvation of Rich Men*, puts this admirably: "Earthly property
should be considered in the light of a staff, an instrument for good
uses."

[2] Luke 12: 16–21.   [3] Luke 9: 25.   [4] Matt. 6: 19–21.

L

It is this danger which lies within wealth that Jesus especially warns men against. It is a simple matter of observation that instead of increasing a man's social sympathies, the struggle for fortune too often makes him selfish and unsocial in that it breaks down that sense of dependence which the poor man feels binding him to other men. In the same proportion as the semblance of independence increases is there danger that a man will forget that he is always an integral part of society and that he can be truly a man only as he is dependent upon God and in sympathy with his fellows. This was the trouble evidently enough with the rich young man of whom we have already spoken. He was endeavoring to build up a perfection upon the corner-stone of a selfish individualism. This is the secret of Jesus' command to trust the Heavenly Father for clothes and food.[1] These things are not evil, but if once regarded as the highest good, they will inevitably lead to a selfish competition for personal advantage at the cost of generous impulses and faith.

With such a conception of the possibilities of humanity as we find in the words of Jesus it would of necessity be impossible that his words

[1] Matt. 6:31–33. See also his warning against covetousness, Luke 12:15.

against those things which are so liable to make
against brotherliness should be sharp and severe.
No man ever had a deeper sympathy with the
poor and unfortunate. He felt profoundly the
misery and injustice which spring from the ir-
responsible power of the wealthy, and sought
with all his strength to arouse new feelings of
philanthropy. In this effort, like all teachers, he
occasionally sought to startle men into a truer
conception of their duties to each other. As
Socrates sometimes played at being a Sophist,
so Jesus sometimes spoke like a fanatic. But in
reality he was farthest possible from fanaticism.
He himself was able to live with poor and rich
alike.[1] If he was homeless, the houses of the
rich were continually at his service. If his head
was sometimes wet with the dews of heaven, he
knew also what it was to have poured upon him
costly ointment. The rich man Zacchæus was
welcomed quite as heartily by him as his fellow-
citizen the beggar Bartimæus. The advice to the
Twelve and the Seventy was evidently due to some

[1] It is a mistake to think of early Christians as altogether from
the poorest classes. They were from the well-to-do and even
wealthy classes as well, as appears not only from the Acts and certain allusions in the epistles, but also from evidence furnished by
the Catacombs. See Rossi, *La Roma Sotteranea Cristiana*; North-
cote and Brownlow, *Roma Sotteranea*.

special cause, for afterwards, when giving them
direction for their entire course of life after his
death, he revoked it, advising a more normal manner of life.[1] Where is there more magnificent
business optimism than his advice to lend money
to those in need, never despairing of its repay-
ment?[2]   Throughout the gospels Jesus never
appears in the garb of an ascetic, for the reason
that he was able to maintain the balance and
perspective of his life.   Indeed his life expresses
even more distinctly than his words the coördi-
nation of his teachings.   All the more weighty
therefore is his judgment upon the unworthy rich.
Wealth he showed to be a good, but a good only
when it is a social good and when its pursuit
does not weaken those impulses within a man
that go out towards his fellows and God, and so
render him unfit for the kingdom of heaven.
Inevitable and fearful punishment awaited the
man whose wealth brought no joy to others than
himself.

V

All this it must be admitted brings Jesus close
to the general position of socialism.   If wealth

[1] Luke 22 : 35, 36.
[2] Luke 6 : 35.   The Authorized Version completely obscures the
thought of Jesus by its arbitrary mistranslation of $\dot{\alpha}\pi\epsilon\lambda\pi\dot{\iota}\zeta o\nu\tau\epsilon s$.

is not for purely individual enjoyment but is to be used for the good of society, and if the ideal society is a brotherhood, it is not a long step to the belief that any form of private property is anti-fraternal and that society itself can best administer economic matters for the good of its members. Something like corroboration is given such an interpretation of Jesus' position by the fact that the company of his followers had a common purse,[1] and that the members of the primitive Jerusalem church "had all things in common."[2]

It is therefore by no means strange that there have always been those who have maintained

[1] John 12:19; 13:6. These texts are so used by Todt, *Der radikale deutsche Socialismus*.

[2] Acts 2:44, 45; 4:32, 36, 37. It is just here that unrhetorical description seems almost beyond hope. For instance, Leslie Stephen (*Social Rights and Duties*, I., 21, 22): "The early Christians were the socialists of their age, and took a view of Dives and Lazarus which would commend itself to the Nihilists of to-day . . . . if the man who best represents the ideas of early Christians were to enter a respectable society of to-day, would it not be likely to send for the police?" A master of clever English like Leslie Stephen has small need of such astonishing nonsense as this to get himself a hearing. Laveleye (*Primitive Property*, Intro. xxxi.), though writing in a different spirit, makes an equally indefensible statement: "If Christianity were taught and understood conformably to the spirit of its Founder, the existing social organism could not last a day."

that in some form of socialism lay the true programme of Christianity. It has repeatedly happened that a revival of faith and zeal has been
accompanied by some doctrine as to community
of goods. "If there were no sin, all temporal
goods would be held in common" has been the
cry of more than one Raymund Lull. The
Waldenses were not singular in going "about
barefoot, two by two, in woollen garments, pos-
sessing nothing, like the apostles."[1] To a considerable degree this is seen beneath the policy
of the great mediæval monastic orders and of
ultra-reformers like some of the Anabaptists.
But in most of these cases their limited communism has been accompanied by more or less asceticism to which the spirit of modern socialism is
radically opposed. No man, however, can bring
any such charge against the Christian socialist of
England, Germany, or America. The great in-
ducement to combine Christianity and socialism
lies along the very different line of their professed
search for greater happiness and completeness
in life, and it cannot be denied that the combination has great attractions. Indeed, if socialism

[1] Quoted by Neander, *History of the Christian Religion and
Church*, IV., 608, from the statement of an eyewitness, the English
Franciscan Walter Mapes.

be only what Maurice[1] declared it to be, "the acknowledgment of brotherhood and fellowship in work," it is but a phase of Christianity.

To think of Jesus as gentle idealist who preached a communism which was neither coarse nor practicable; to see in the Jerusalem church a group of kindred idealists attempting to practise the same unworldly economy; to see only sophistry in the word of any man who ventures to think that the early church fathers did not regard riches as the fruit of usurpation; all this is captivating, but it will hardly bear severer scrutiny than the less euphemistic "Le bon sansculotte," of Camille Desmoulins.[2]

For it is futile to attempt to discover modern socialism in the words of Jesus. There is, it is true, nothing incompatible with such a system were it once proved to be the means best adapted to furthering the true spirit of brotherliness; but

[1] *Life*, II., 128.

[2] So Nitti, *Le Socialisme Catholique*, especially chs. ii., iii. Less learned but equally extreme views are constantly to be met. For instance, R. Heber Newton, *Social Studies*, 332 *sq*. It is gratifying to find an opposite view presented in so important a work as Nathusius, *Die Mitarbeit der Kirche an der Lösung der Socialen Frage*, II., 274 *sq*. As one would expect, thorough historians reject the idea of there having been communism in the Jerusalem church. For instance, Weizsäcker, *History of the Apostolic Age* (Eng. ed.), I., 56. See also Keim, *Jesus of Nazara*, III., 345–347.

just as true is it that there is nothing incompatible with a rational individualism.   One can sympathize heartily with Maurice and Kingsley as they denounce grinding competition or a supposed "iron law of wages," but as a follower of Jesus one stands committed to neither socialism nor individualism.   Before either is declared unchristian it must be shown to be hopelessly opposed to the accomplishment of Jesus' ideal order.   Charity, with Jesus, is not communism.   If it could be proved that he had been an Essene, the identification might be easier, but that possibility is now little thought of.[1]   Probably no one would soberly commit Jesus to communism because of Judas and the bag, and so far as any direct word or single act of his is concerned, it is necessary to say the same.   Even in the case of the primitive Jerusalem church it is impossible to discover anything like communism in the modern sense of the word. Its members, be they never so rich, were not required to sell their possessions and to give to the poor, if we are to accept the words of Peter to Ananias.[2]   Indeed, the story of Ananias and

[1] See Godet, *Commentary on Luke;* Lightfoot, *Commentary on the Epistle to the Colossians,* Appendix; Renan, *History of the People of Israel,* V., 48–66.

[2] Acts 4 : 4.

Sapphira does not make their fate dependent upon
their failure to share all their property, but upon
their lying to the effect that they had so done.
Nor does it appear that all the members of the
church at Jerusalem disposed of their property,
since the mother of Mark had her own house.[1]
As a matter of fact, it would seem that this sharing of wealth in Jerusalem was simply an expression of natural enthusiasm and Christian love. It
may, perhaps, have involved a too literal interpretation of Jesus' words, but even this is by no
means clear. At any rate, a few years after this
so-called communism we find the church at Jerusalem counselling, not communism, but generosity
to the poor,[2] and the "contribution for the poor
among the saints in Jerusalem" replacing the
"having of things in common."[3] If there really
had ever been any communism, its outcome was a
reductio ad absurdum — a commentary upon the
words of Jesus that will repay reflection.[4]

In the matter of charity we find Jesus expressing by his life the common sense that is to be

---

[1] Acts 12 : 12.   [2] Gal. 2 : 9.   [3] Rom. 15 : 26.

[4] " What means would be left of communicating one to another,
if none had the means to bestow " (*i.e.* had given everything away)?
asks Clement of Alexandria, who doubtless saw that the Christians
of Alexandria needed little encouragement to engage in business if
the words of the Emperior Hadrian to his brother-in-law, Servia-

used in the interpretation of his more radical
statements.   When his friends saw fit to criticise
a woman who had anointed him, on the ground
that the cost of the ointment might much better
have been given to the poor, Jesus rebukes
them, though using those words which so often
have incited to charity, "The poor ye have with
you always, that when ye will ye may do them
good." [1]   There was a duty higher than charity.
It would, indeed, be far less correct to say that
Jesus taught indiscriminate giving than to say
that according to his general principle of love,
charity would at times be forbidden as hurtful
rather than helpful.

Nor did Jesus approach that form of socialism
that would equalize the sharing of products.   On
the contrary, when using commercial matters as
illustrations he did not condemn competition, and
in one instance he distinctly recognized the principle of difference in rewards.   "Unto him that
hath shall be given" [2] comes with ill grace from
a socialist.   The parable of the market-place has
no economic force; but if it had, equality in

nus, are correct. Speaking of the inhabitants of Alexandria he
says, "They have all of them but one God — money; 'tis he alone
that Christians, Jews, and all the rest adore."

[1] Matt. 26 : 6–11.   [2] Matt. 25 : 29.

wages is not its point, but the owner's right to
do as he saw fit with his own property.[1] Farthest
possible was Jesus from the curse of most social-
istic programmes — the assumption that the ideal
social order is based upon an increase in creature
comforts. If there is anything unchristian, it is
the notion that bread and amusements and good
drainage are going to bring in the millennium.
The same Jesus that fed the multitude withstood
the temptation to use his higher powers to satisfy mere hunger, and deliberately alienated those
who sought to exploit his philanthropy while
refusing his teaching.[2]

VI

The translation of this central teaching of Jesus
into modern phrase is by no means difficult, although at this point temptation to over-emphasis
is very strong. Jesus was not an economist, and
had little interest in abstract questions. His
position at bottom was practical. The search
for wealth is a moral matter and its use is also
a moral matter. If one cannot be faithful in the
unrighteous mammon, he is unfit to be entrusted
with the true riches. Wealth is a public trust —
a principle that is made no less true from the

[1] Matt. 20 : 17.   [2] John 6 : 26, 27, 66.

fact that its application to the various problems
of any age must be left to the age itself. As
in the teaching of Jesus in regard to the state,
the first point to be settled is as to whether an
existing economic institution or custom or effort
tends to the establishment of fraternity. If it
does not, the face of Christ is against it, and the
only escape from his woe is to abolish whatever
keeps its possessor from using it or producing it
to the advantage of society. For such minds as
would regard this as an ethical platitude, Jesus
furnishes abundant stimulus in the sayings of the
Sermon on the Mount. For those who itch less
for sensational novelties, this teaching of Jesus
will furnish the point of departure for any economic philosophy that cares to use his name.

To be more specific, Jesus was neither a syco-
phant nor a demagogue. He neither forbids
trusts nor advises them; he is neither a champion nor an opponent of *laissez faire;* he neither
forbids trades unions, strikes and lock-outs, nor
advises them; he was neither socialist nor indi-
vidualist. Jesus was a friend neither of the working man nor the rich man as such. The question
he would put to a man is not "Are you rich?"
but "Have you done the will of my Father?"
He calls the poor man to sacrifice as well as the

rich man. He was the Son of Man, not the son of a class of men. But his denunciation is unsparing of those men who make wealth at the expense of souls; who find in capital no incentive to further fraternity; who endeavor so to use wealth as to make themselves independent of social obligations and to grow fat with that which should be shared with society; — for those men who are gaining the world but are letting their neighbors fall among thieves and Lazarus rot among their dogs.

CHAPTER VII

SOCIAL LIFE

It is not difficult to see that the principle of fraternity must especially apply to those forms of social life outside the family circle which are neither political nor economic. In nothing do the better instincts of modern life more strenuously exert themselves than in the attempt so to adjust social relations that the chasms caused by differences in wealth and culture may be, if not abolished, at least bridged. Almost in the same proportion as one comes under their control do altruistic motives result in revolt against conventional distinctions, and an attempt at brotherliness, or at least neighborliness. This is at least one interpretation to be put upon not only socialism, but upon our new charitable movements and organizations and especially upon social settlements. Confessedly these new motives are Christian; nothing could be more so; but it may not be without results to follow the application of his general principle to social matters made by Jesus himself.

I

It may seem gratuitous to assert that Jesus was no ascetic or even semi-ascetic puritan. So far has the pendulum swung away from the mediæval conception of holiness that it often seems as if the chief need of to-day were a Savonarola who should fascinate the nineteenth century into new burnings of novels and gewgaws. But none the less, so ineradicable is the suspicion that religion is in some way a sort of counter-agent for the joys of life, that it is often forgotten that the founder of Christianity came eating and drinking, in the envious eyes of contemporary religious teachers a winebibber and a glutton.[1] It was in fact because he was so normal that Jesus' career was darkened by men's distrust. John the Baptist, whose work in a fashion Jesus may be said to have continued and completed, was quite another man. The prophet's dress and the pauper's food together with his sternly ascetic preaching gave him a popularity and a position among the Jews which Jesus during his life can hardly be said to have attained.[2] Even nowadays it

---

[1] Matt. 11 : 19.

[2] The hold that John had upon the minds of his contemporaries is to be seen not only in the oldest sources of our gospels (see for

is by no means so easy to attract the crowds by respectability as by eccentricity and sensations. It is infinitely easier to preach against fashionable extravagances and social absurdities than to recall men to gentlemanly unobtrusiveness in goodness. Too many men yet measure their goodness by their sense of deprivation, making misery the thermometer of holiness.

But Jesus was evidently not of this class of charlatans and semi-ascetics. It cannot have escaped the notice of even the conventional reader of the New Testament that in the Fourth Gospel Jesus begins his Galilean ministry by providing a wedding company with new means for enjoyment.[1] And this was only one instance out of many in which Jesus used social gatherings for the furthering of his mission. In fact much of his teaching was connected with

instance Mark 1: 1–8) but also in the pages of Josephus (*Ant.* 18; 5: 2). By the latter writer the misfortunes that filled the later days of Herod Antipas are said to have been popularly regarded as judgments for the killing of John. Even if, as very likely is the case, this reference to John has been subjected to interpolations, it stands on much securer critical ground than Josephus' reference to Jesus himself (*Ant.* 18; 3: 3). Other tributes to the permanence of John's influence are seen in Acts 18: 25; 19: 3.

[1] John 2: 1–12. It is impossible to think that the conditions of this story are fulfilled by the assumption that the wine provided by Jesus was non-alcoholic.

dining, the social meal giving either the occasion or the analogy for his thought. He distinctly rejected fasting as a religious form,[1] and destroyed all ceremonial distinctions in food.[2] If sometimes he himself fasted,[3] it was from no desire to acquire merit, and if he withdrew into solitude it was for a brief season of prayer from which he returned the more devotedly to enter into public life.[4] For months he lived almost constantly surrounded by crowds.

But while the pleasures of social life are good in themselves, they are not to be ends in themselves. Life consists in something more than food,[5] and the kingdom of God, as Paul said later, was not to consist in mere sensual enjoyment.[6] That something which can make eating and drinking goods subordinate to some greater good is the spirit of brotherliness in which they become means of furthering the happiness of others. The member of the new society was not to flee the world,[7] but was rather to stay in it as a source of light and life.[8] Social life

---

[1] Matt. 9 : 14; 6 : 17, 18. In this connection his picture of the boasting Pharisee (Luke 18 : 10) is especially striking.

[2] Mark 7 : 17, 19.   [3] Matt. 4 : 12; Luke 4 : 2.

[4] Mark 6 : 46 *sq.*; Matt. 14 : 23 *sq.*; Luke 9 : 28.

[5] Matt. 6 : 25.   [7] John 17 : 15.

[6] Rom. 14 : 17.   [8] Matt. 5 : 14.

M

was shown both by the words and life of Jesus to be the normal life of men. Just as marriage was the ideal form of the life of the individual, so the family and the feast were used by Jesus as the nearest analogies to what life in the new social order was to be. Friendships are to Jesus' mind instinctive and their fruit of necessity, kindliness.[1]

II

It is not to magnify trivialities if attention be called to the attitude of Jesus towards the conventionalities of life. It is of course possible that a man should be thoroughly good and worthy of respect and yet be totally indifferent to the requirements of society. Many men to-day are undoubtedly nobly affecting the life of their communities through their sterling integrity and deep religious feeling who are ignorant or careless of conventionalities. But no cultured man wants a boor as his religious teacher any more than he would accept a filthy saint as his Saviour. Even John the Baptist was less than the least in the kingdom of God.[2] And it is nothing more than we should have expected when we find Jesus careful about those matters which indicate the gentleman. Though a poor

[1] Luke 11: 5-8; 15: 9.   [2] Matt. 11: 11.

man and counting clothes as at best but a secondary good[1] he seems to have been well dressed[2] and to have followed the ordinary dictates of the Jewish fashions except, perhaps, in the matter of phylacteries.[3] His sensitiveness to matters of common civility appears in the words forced from him by the rudeness of a host who allowed conceit to drive out politeness.[4] Indeed it would seem as if the fact that Judas should have betrayed him by a kiss added bitterness to the cup he was forced to drink.[5]

These matters are, of course, of small importance as they stand by themselves, but they gain in significance when they are seen to represent an attitude of mind. Conduct is always less hypocritical than language, and in the case of Jesus it had the added responsibility of serving as an example for his followers. Accordingly, it is

---

[1] Matt. 6: 25, 28. [2] John 19: 23.

[3] Matt. 9: 20. The rabbis seem to have been as supreme in fashion as in religion. We know from their decisions not only the names and styles of the garments worn by Jews but also the order in which they should be put on and their relative importance. (The authority on the subject of Jewish costume is Brüll, *Trachten der Juden.* See also Edersheim, *Life and Times of Jesus the Messiah,* I., 621 *sq.*) The fact to be especially noticed in this connection is the probability that Jesus wore the *tsitsith* or tassels on his *tallith* or outer garment.

[4] Luke 7 : 36–50. [5] Luke 22 : 48.

doubly necessary in his case to look for the spirit and ideal of which conduct is the expression.

But at the same time that he conformed to the ordinary habits of polite society as he knew it, whether it may have been from sensitiveness or from some other motive, Jesus, with all his love and eagerness to attract men, never cheapened himself by indiscriminate friendships. From one point of view, his brief career was marked by great reserve; indeed, it seems hardly more than a series of withdrawals from men in order that he might establish a few intense friendships. To the outer crowd he carefully refused to show the depths of his character; to the wide circle of mercurial "believers" he revealed hardly more of himself; to the Twelve as a whole he showed as much of himself as he could educate them to appreciate. But when he found a man or woman to whom he could open his heart, then all that they wished to receive of him was theirs to receive. His joys and his sorrows alike might be shared by them. Some men are at their best in public; others, among their intimates. The first come dangerously near acting; the latter are seldom insincere. Jesus belonged emphatically to the second class. While he knew something of the intoxicating

joy that comes to the orator, his choicest teachings are those given in some conversation. He
would not cast his pearls before swine.[1] Thus
it came about that while he was followed by
multitudes, he was loved by only a few.

III

But because he thus chose his companions, it
would be absurd to say that Jesus recognizes the
existence of social classes in the new order of
society. His limitations of intimacy were not
based upon accidental differences. Nor do his
teachings imply such classes. Such anomalies
as exist within an unhealthy society were naturally impossible within a society composed of normal men. So long as men were bad, so long
they could not be other than selfish. All of
their efforts could be only for private advantage.
Wealth could not fail to be other than a means
for ungenerous enjoyment.[2] Prayer would lengthen
itself immoderately that the Creator might be
wearied into submission to the more persistent
will.[3] Social customs would be only new agencies
for forcing an indebted acquaintance to repay
hospitality in kind.[4] Jesus saw all this clearly;

---

[1] Matt. 7 : 6.   [3] Matt. 7 : 7.
[2] Luke 12 : 16–21.   [4] Luke 14 : 12.

and he saw its inevitable outgrowth : the stratification of men according to their ability to fulfil
these purely materialistic conditions. With such
stratification fraternity would be impossible. Therefore he who attempted to exalt himself would
be humiliated.[1] In the kingdom no man was to
be called master, for they were all brethren,[2]
serving one another. And not only were they
brothers one of another, they were his brothers
as well, the least as well as the greatest. No
more striking lesson of social equality was ever
given than that of the Christ going about with
a towel washing the feet of his followers.[3] So
emphatically does Jesus preach the gospel of
equality as to say that in the coming order, the
last should be first, and the first last.[4]

Yet he does not, like some modern champions
of the doctrine, attempt the sudden destruction
of all traditional distinctions. There is undoubtedly need of such iconoclasts, for reforms
like revolutions are seldom made of rose-water,
but that constructive spirit which is everywhere
noticeable in the career of Jesus is present here

---

[1] Matt. 23 : 12.   [2] Matt. 23 : 8.   [3] John 13 : 1–10.
[4] Matt. 19 : 30. No sentence of Jesus seems to have made
deeper impression on his hearers. It is constantly repeated in the
gospels.

in large measure. Social revolutions quite as likely as political produce demagogues, and even more quickly tempt men to denunciations that are the more violent because more indiscriminate. But Jesus kept himself from all such extremes. He himself belonged to the artisan class,[1] and knew what it was to feel the contempt of the professional teachers of his people,[2] and he did not hesitate to confess the immense advantage possessed by the educated man,[3] but he never allowed these facts to lead him into tirade against other men's advantages.

It is, however, by no means inconsistent with this attitude that he recognized, that as things are constituted, men must of necessity be divided into servants and employés. He said nothing that condemned such a relation, and indeed at times spoke of it as a most natural thing.[4] But this is simply the attitude that any practical man must take in his reforming of society. Your amateur reformer would dissolve society into its elements. Like Robespierre and other doctrinaires, he will break with the past, even though he brings the bones of departed kings to the lime-pit. But Jesus was never so crude a thinker as to imagine

---

[1] Mark 6: 3.
[2] Matt. 13: 54–56.
[3] Matt. 13: 52.
[4] Luke 17: 7–10; Matt. 10: 24.

that society is a mechanical mixture of elements
into which it must be disintegrated as a step
towards a happier recombination. With him
progress was biological, an evolution rather than
a revolution. And therefore he did not destroy
all social conventionalities or a traditional division
of labor.

But to be a servant is not to be any less a man
or, provided it is really the case, any less the equal
of any man in another calling. If nothing that
goes into a man can defile him, certainly no necessary work is dishonorable. If Jesus the carpenter and the son of a carpenter could become
Jesus the Christ; if his seemingly Falstaffian
army of fishermen, tax-collectors, and reformed
revolutionists could become in a few months the
pillars of the great church at Jerusalem and the
evangelists of the world; it is unnecessary to
argue as to Jesus' recognition of the equality of
men as men. Indeed, nothing is more admirable
than the catholicity of sympathy and practice that
made him the friend of all sorts of people. Yet
nothing more scandalized the aristocratic teachers
and preachers and lawyers of his own day. How
often did they rail against him as a friend of the
publican and the sinner! In their sight he could
be no prophet, since he dared receive a repentant

woman of the town.[1] With them as with all
legalists the temptation was strong to judge
harshly and superficially of all unusual characters,
and their criticism of the generous habits of Jesus
was a testimony to the openness of his sympathy
with honest effort at reform and his disregard of
all artificial distinctions. To the Pharisees the
common people who knew not the law were ac-
cursed: to Jesus they were possible members of
his kingdom.[2] He knew of no "lower classes."

And his words were the echoes of his life. One
of the proofs of his Messiahship that the disciples
of John were to carry back to their unfortunate
master was that the gospel was being preached to
the poor.[3] As he himself ate with the publican
and the sinner, so when a man would give a feast,
Jesus bade him invite the lame and the halt and
the blind.[4] Could social equality combined with
an avoidance of self-seeking be more strikingly
enforced?

IV

Various objections may be urged to this conception of Jesus as a preacher of social equality.

It may be said that he discriminated against
Samaritans and heathen, holding both himself and

[1] Luke 7: 39 *sq.*   [3] Matt. 11: 5; Luke 7: 22.
[2] John 7: 49; Matt. 11: 28.   [4] Luke 14: 12 *sq.*

his disciples straitly to a mission to "the lost sheep of the house of Israel."[1]   Yet even assuming (which is quite gratuitous) that such a distinction is a distinction between social classes, it would be enough to reply that such a limitation was but a concentration.   As the results showed, it was eminent sagacity that forbade the dissipation of energy and the extension of preaching by men not yet thoroughly imbued with his own spirit.   In the plans of Jesus the evangelization of Jerusalem was to lead to that of Judea and Samaria and ultimately of the uttermost parts of the earth.[2]   But as a more immediate reply it would be sufficient to match the story of Zacchæus[3] with that of the Syro-Phœnician woman;[4] and the words to the Twelve as they went out to a final conquest of the world with the advice given to them as they made their first experiment at heralding a disappointing Jewish Messiah.

It may be also urged that Jesus attacked the rich and educated classes and championed the poor.   But such attacks and championings are rather proofs of his equalizing purpose.   Princes were to be put down from their thrones and those of low degree were to be exalted,[5] not that in

---

[1] Matt. 10:6; 15:24.   [3] Luke 19:2 *sq.*   [5] Luke 1:52, 53.
[2] Acts 1:8.   [4] Mark 7:24 *sq.*

their new conditions they might perpetuate old distinctions, but that it might be made evident that personality and not position or wealth is supreme. Equality with Jesus was not to be attained by equalizing wealth or honor, but by the possession of a common divine life, the enjoyment of equal privileges, and the performance of equal duties. It is moral, not material.

It is true that Jesus attacked bitterly the upper classes, and at times seemed unduly to praise the poor and needy, but it is a superficial study that does not discover that these attacks spring from his perception of the evident anti-fraternal, selfish, contemptuous spirit of the aristocrats. Notwithstanding his intense sympathy with the poor and miserable, in none of his words is there a touch of demagogism. A man was no more the worse because he was rich than he was the holier because he was miserable. Indeed, if there is anything that projects above the other teachings of Jesus it is the duty of every member of the kingdom of God to treat every man as his equal. This was to be not a mere social fiction but a test of devotion and character. "By this shall all men know that ye are my disciples if ye love one another."[1] To be a neighbor to a man is

[1] John 13: 35.

not to belong to the same community, or set, or nation. It is to disregard all such artificial distinctions and to give him such help as he may need.[1] He who has such a spirit will ever be the Good Samaritan and to him every sufferer will be the man fallen among robbers.

Yet probably the strongest objection in the way of an actual recognition of this ideal of Jesus in actual life is the ineradicable conviction that social equality is impracticable. Men have dreamed of it and have died, leaving their dreams to the laughter of their times and the libraries of their descendants. These words of Jesus are beautiful, but so are those of More and Rousseau — and no more visionary. Men are not equal and fraternity is a word for orators and French public buildings.

So men say, or think if they keep silent.

But Jesus does not claim that men in the world to-day are physiologically equal. There are the lame and halt. Nor are they mentally on an equality. There are men to whom one talent could be entrusted, and those to whom five and ten.[2] Nor does Jesus so far fall into the class of nature-philosophers as to teach that because men are to be brothers they are therefore to be twins. The equality of fraternity does not con-

[1] Luke 10: 25-37.   [2] Matt. 25: 14-30; Luke 19: 12-27.

sist in duplication of powers, but in the enjoyment and the exercise of love.

Further, according to the new social standard of Jesus two men are equal, not because they have equal claims upon each other, but because they owe equal duties to each other. The gospel is not a new Declaraton of Rights, but a Declaration of Duties.[1]

V

As to what equality shall consist in when the perfect social order is attained, Jesus gives us no clear teaching. But one can safely infer that it would not be uniformity. Men would then be brothers and society an all-embracing family, but individuality is not to be lost. And individuality is synonymous with personal inequalities.

But this is a speculation into which Jesus did not enter. He is especially concerned with the evolving kingdom, and here his words are explicit. Social and economic distinctions are artificial and temporary. Differences in wealth and employment are to be no hindrance to frater-

[1] The constitutional history of the French Revolution is a commentary upon this position of Jesus. It was a new age that replaced the *Declaration des Droits de l'Homme et du Citoyen* of the constitution of 1791, with the *Declaration des Droits et ces Devoirs de l'Homme et du Citoyen* of the constitution of Fructidor, 1795.

nity.[1] To use the noble words of Paul, who here again seems more than all men of the first century to have reached the heart of Jesus, in the new social order "there can be neither Jew nor Greek, there can be neither bond nor free." [2] Has the world quite proved that this is impossible?

---

[1] Such was to a surprising extent the spirit of the early church. Almost no titles are to be found among the oldest inscriptions in the Catacombs of St. Calixtus. And Lactantius pleads, "With us there is no difference between the poor and the rich, the slave and the free man. We call ourselves brothers because we believe ourselves equal."

[2] Gal. 3 : 28.

CHAPTER VIII

THE FORCES OF HUMAN PROGRESS

It is comparatively easy to construct an ideal for society, but it is rare that the reformer sufficiently considers the applicability of his ideal to actual human nature. It is this that has made an archæological puzzle of Plato's Republic and a romance of Utopia. Men instinctively feel that no dream of a regenerate society is worth serious consideration that does not in some distinct way show its ability, as Carlyle would say, "to walk." Jesus cannot escape such a test. If his ideal is worth anything, and if his teachings are to be anything more than a collection of oriental apothegms, he must be seen to have approached the problems of human progress with a full conception of the inertia of life and the repugnance most men show towards anything like social effort. In other words, Jesus must be required to set forth with reasonable fulness the forces upon which he counted for the realization of his new social order. We ask of him not merely an ideal, but a method.

I

If, in a search for a recognition on Jesus' part of such forces, one comes to the memorabilia of his life fresh from the study of modern efforts at social regeneration, nothing is more surprising than the forces in human society upon which he does not count.

It is of course to be expected that he should distinctly refuse to use mere physical force as a means of establishing his kingdom.[1] A Mahomet may rule as a prophet in a kingdom of Allah built upon the sword, but a Jesus cannot. A Charlemagne may build an empire from Saxons who have chosen baptism as a lesser evil than death, but not so the followers of him whose kingdom was not of this world.[2] The new social order was to be spiritual, not material.

But it is less to be anticipated that Jesus should have so passed over those claims for justice which to-day are urged with an ever-increasing passion. It would not do to say that Jesus is oblivious to the rightful claims of those who have not shared sufficiently in the good things

[1] Matt. 4:10, 11; John 6:15.   [2] John 18:36.

of life. No man's teaching has been more po-
tent in forcing the strong to yield to the weak,
the rich to the poor, the noble to the lowly.
But none the less is it true that Jesus is far
less interested in the rights than in the obligations of men. It matters little that logically the
two conceptions are complementary. Practically
there is a vast difference between the bald demand of men or classes for things due them, and
that extension of privilege which sympathy and
a sense of obligation may induce a favored man
or class to effect. Of the two, it is easier to
inculcate justice, but no one who knows the
crimes that have been committed in the name
of liberty, and the hereditary hatreds that have
been the outgrowth of struggles after rights,
need be told that the victories of justice leave
scars as ineradicable as its demands are righteous. It was from some appreciation of this
that Jesus made duty paramount to rights. The
Jew was ready enough to grant the rights of a
neighbor — when once neighborship had been
defined and proved. In the estimation of Jesus
to be a neighbor was not to have rights that
put others under obligation to oneself, but to be
conscious of duties. Not the wounded traveller,
but the Levite and the priest and the Samaritan

N

needed to show the spirit of the neighbor.[1] Indeed, to one who has been assailed loudly with
the evils of to-day's economic inequalities, it is
at first sight surprising to find Jesus so indifferent to much that to-day's reformers emphasize
so strenuously. The ordinary appeal which we
hear addressed to the wage-earner nowadays
seems a paraphrase of Proudhon's "property is
robbery." The poor man is urged to get a larger
share in the wealth he helps produce; to cease
to be a horse that drags the coach in which the
rich folk ride. Now, again, the position of
Jesus in regard to wealth puts him here uncom-
promisingly upon the side of the man who has
not shared justly in the distribution of the products of labor and capital. But to urge the poor
man to struggle after wealth might be to spur
him to selfishness as deep as that of the rich
man against whom he struggles. It might be
necessary to subdue nature, to make natural
forces the servants of production, but wealth
and sensuousness and selfishness, Jesus saw, go
hand in hand.[2] Mere bigness is not goodness,
and enthusiasm over bank accounts is not the
spirit of the Master. The kingdom did not
come with observation.[3] Life was more than

[1] Luke 10 : 25-37.   [2] Luke 8 : 14.   [3] Luke 17 : 20.

food and fraternity more than wealth.[1]   Social
agitators, John the Baptists of economics, are
needed; we may yet count Karl Marx and
Lassalle among the prophets, but what sort of
kingdom would a Christ have established whose
evangel was a political economy and whose new
age was set forth in a programme?

Nor does Jesus appeal to the æsthetic side
of men's nature.   It is no sign of disloyalty to
beauty and the educational function of art, to say
that the world yet waits the advent of an æsthetic
philosophy whose guarantee of constant progress
can be accepted.   As in the case of the demand
for economic justice, so in the case of an exclusive
appeal to the love of beauty, selfishness crouches
at the door.   To say nothing of the fact that
comparatively few men are susceptible to any
persistent moral impulse from the æsthetic side
of their natures, the call to be beautiful and
to love that which is beautiful is not made of
the stuff that makes heroes and martyrs.   It is
indispensable as a subsidiary motive, and as
such at least Jesus seems to have recognized
it,[2] but from the days of beauty-mad Greece, an
æsthetic spirit has failed to develop a long-
lived, virile, generous civilization.   The apostle

[1] Luke 12:23.   [2] Matt. 6:28.

of culture finds his case weak, in fact hopeless, if mingled with the æsthetic conception of the Greek there be not the stern Hebrew sense of right and God.

It goes without saying that Jesus does not base his hopes of a new society upon an "enlightened self-interest," or any other hedonist philosophy. That the individual would seek his own good he seems to have assumed,[1] and he never hesitated to appeal to humanity's hopes and fears. But that this in any way needed excuse, or that it was necessary to raise this natural impulse into a philosophy and reduce all social service to terms of a whitewashed selfishness, seems never to have occurred to him. No man ever struck out more manfully against both self-depreciation and self-exaltation than Jesus, but the motive upon which he expected men to act was not that of the improvement of the individual atom. Self-preservation may be the final motive of physical nature, but not with the followers of Jesus. "Whosoever will save his life shall lose it."[2]

Taken altogether, it is obvious that the forces upon which Jesus relied to make his ideal society an actual fact in life, were neither mechanical nor selfish. Whatever approach society as he found

[1] Matt. 7:12; Luke 6:31.   [2] Matt. 16:25.

it was to make towards that better order which he described would not be the result of external propulsion or of calculation. As the kingdom of God is spiritual, so are the forces which bring about its realization; and as it is a family, so are its members to be not self-seekers, but brothers.

II

If, now, we attempt more positively to set forth those primary forces upon which Jesus counted for the accomplishment of his ideals, we are forced back upon his fundamental conception of the nature of man. Jesus trusts the inherent powers and capacities of the race. The ideal he portrays was not intended for creatures less or more human than the men with whom he associated and out of whom he hoped to form his kingdom. Individual and social regeneration is possible because man and society are inherently salvable. And deep in the heart of a humanity that could be saved were its wants. Not that he ever formally classifies them. Indeed he can hardly be said to recognize all their categories. But nevertheless he presupposes them. In his estimation they are in themselves morally neutral, yet according to the relative importance assigned to each of them they may express either a healthy or decadent person-

ality.   It is in this perspective in which he sees
the various wants of men that Jesus shows the
instinct of the practical man and not that of the
fanatic.   Thus in the case of purely physical
wants, with a characteristic loyalty to his anti-
ascetic ideals, Jesus assumes the legitimacy of the
child's cry for food,[1] bids his disciples pray for
bread,[2] and pities a multitude which he saw grow
faint with hunger.[3]   Yet physical wants are inferior
to many others.   Man is not to live by bread
alone,[4] and spiritual intensity might altogether
lift one, as it did himself, quite above mere physical
hunger.[5]   One of the sharpest rebukes he ever
administered to his disciples was occasioned by
their crass misinterpretation of one of his sayings
as a caution against certain classes of bakers from
whom they might be tempted to buy bread.[6]   The
same is true of all economic wants.   Who better
than Jesus ever appreciated the power of a mer-
chant's desire to succeed in business,[7] or of a
laborer's passion for a larger wage?[8]   The Heavenly Father knows his children have need of food
and raiment,[9] but just for that very reason men

[1] Matt. 7 : 9.

[2] Matt. 6 : 11.

[3] Matt. 15 : 32; Mark 8 : 3.

[4] Matt. 4 : 4.

[5] John 4 : 31–34.

[6] Matt. 16 : 5–12; Mark 8 : 14–21.

[7] Matt. 13 : 45.

[8] Matt. 20 : 2 *sq.*

[9] Matt. 6 : 31, 32; John 6 : 27.

are not to make the search for them the chief end
in life. A man's life does not consist in the
abundance of things that he possesses.[1]

The satisfaction, not of these lower wants, but of
those other and higher desires after truth and the
higher verities and experiences of life, is to be the
underlying motive in the new order of life.   Men
are not to be compelled to be good, but their desires
are to lead them to goodness, or, if the desire be
lacking, are to be convinced of the sin of the lack.[2]
Not obedience, but loving impulse, is the key to
noble living.   The members of his new society are
to be not servants but friends,[3] and conventional
duties are no measure of what friendship may
prompt.[4]

Chief among these basal desires of men Jesus
would class the desire to know God. To know
him not merely as a truth or principle, but as
a person.   The cry of Philip, "Show us the

[1] Luke 12 : 15.

[2] John 16 : 8-10. In this connection one recalls the eagerness
with which Jesus met an honest seeker after truth like Nathaniel
and Thomas, Zacchæus and Martha, as well as the earnestness, not
to say severity, with which he answered those whose ignorance was
in part due to their own failure to follow their better instincts, as
Nicodemus and Philip. Compare also the philosophy by which the
Fourth Gospel accounts for the presence or absence of the faith
that accepts Jesus. John 3 : 18-21.

[3] John 15 : 15.   [4] Luke 17 : 10.

Father," [1] was the outburst of humanity's heart, and the answer it drew forth has satisfied generations. The chief significance of the life of Jesus may be said in the light of history to have lain in himself rather than in his teaching. He was the revealer of God. So his contemporaries judged him, though at first but dimly. So the second century thought of him exclusively.[2] And although Jesus does not describe with any detail the nature of this want of a more perfect knowledge of God, and treats it more as a need than as a desire, it is always present as a postulate controlling his preaching and life.[3] He had come that men might receive the divine life more abundantly.[4]

And similarly in regard to the relations existing between men themselves, Jesus, while never analyzing the psychology of ethics, addresses himself to that which was even more sadly evident in his day than in ours, men's need of some standard

[1] John 14 : 8.

[2] If there were need, reference might here be made to the epistles of Clement of Rome and Barnabas, but the fact is so uniformly admitted that argument seems gratuitous. How deep an impression this conception of Jesus had made by the very beginning of the second century is to be seen in our Fourth Gospel.

[3] This is especially felt in reading the Fourth Gospel. Thus, John 6 : 57; 17 : 1-26.

[4] John 10 : 10.

and motive for better dealings with their fellows. For this reason it was, that, according to the oldest sources of our gospel, he received so sympathetically the rich young man who desired to be perfect,[1] and the lawyer who could appreciate the summation of Mosaism in the double command to love God and man.[2] These men were no mere tricksters, but seekers after a more definite ethical standard. And doubtless it was in large measure for the same reason that the multitudes for a while hung upon his words. He would not be a judge and a divider in matters of property,[3] but he taught freely in regard to social duties, as he saw men needed his instruction. And it mattered nothing whether the want was in a hasty woman,[4] a timid son,[5] or over-zealous disciples.[6]

Still, the questions return: the duty he set before men furnished the standard for life — did it also in any way furnish the motive for more rational social life ? Granting that men do want, or at least need a knowledge of God and a better ethical standard, how does Jesus proceed to turn the need into motive ? Was he, after all, but

[1] Mark 10: 17–31.
[2] Mark 12: 28–34.
[3] Luke 12: 13–15.

[4] Luke 10: 38–42.
[5] Matt. 18: 21, 22.
[6] Mark 9: 38 *sq*.

another in the list of noble men who have commanded men to love but who have not made love easy?

If we revert once more to Christ's conception of man, we see the basis of this double need. Man is a social being who finds his normal life only in union. It is the imperfect union that causes unrest. Jesus but deepened the need when he revealed the normal life of men; a life which, as has already appeared, involves a twofold social relationship; a divine sonship and a human fraternity. These are the sources of the Christian motives that inevitably make toward the building up of both individual and society.

III

It is not necessary again to discuss what Jesus meant by the terms "father" and "son" as he used them to describe the relations that may and should exist between man and God. It will be enough to consider how the supreme relationship they express may furnish motives for social life.

The revelation of the possibility of the divine sonship of man by Jesus becomes the source of motive power in two particulars.

As in the case of all ideals, the revelation of

the possibilities of human life made by the character and life of Jesus himself stirred men's hearts to emulation and duplication.   But Jesus never represents himself in the fashion of the Stoic, strong enough in his own unaided virtue to conquer sin within and difficulty without.   His was a life of prayer.[1]   He did always the will of his Father.[2]   The depths of his life were united with the Divine.[3]   He and his Father are one.   In these particulars Jesus has always been an inspiration for all those who have studied his life. Men who are dubious about the historic records of his life, nevertheless are anxious to see this ideal type of character more and more reproduced in themselves.[4]   And whatever may have been the explanations of his influence given by others, in Jesus' own mind the highest result that could come from his intercourse with his disciples was

[1] Matt. 14 : 23; Luke 5 : 16; Mark 1 : 35; Luke 6 : 12; 9 : 28; John 14 : 16; 16 : 26; Matt. 26 : 36.

[2] John 6 : 39 ; 8 : 29; Matt 26 : 42.

[3] John 10 : 30.   This is also the clear implication of the stories of the baptism.   Matt. 3 : 13–17; Luke 3 : 21, 22; John 1 : 32–34. How quickly this oldest conception of Jesus passed on the one hand into a confusion of his person with that of the Father and on the other into a mechanical conception of his power, may be seen in the literature of the second century.   Compare, for instance, the Epistle of Barnabas with the Gospel of Peter.

[4] Sheldon, *An Ethical Movement*, p. 123.

their sharing in this complete life; a life that should satisfy their nature's demands for a life united with God; a life in which they were one with themselves, with him, and with his Father.[1]

Yet the results of this new relationship — this sonship — were after all the fundamental things with Jesus. As his example was calculated to lead men to something other than an atomistic, self-centred moral life (if such a thing is conceivable), so the new sonship would result in new moral impulses, new moral states, out of which might rise new motives and choices. And this was the condition of entering the kingdom — a man was to be born again.[2] "He that hath the Son hath the life."[3]

The older theologians seldom failed to read the words of Jesus at this point with unanimity,[4] and that too while tending to displace the psychological fact with forensic justification. Nothing is nearer the heart of the teaching of both Jesus and Paul than the moral change that is the result of the interpenetration of the human

---

[1] John 17 : 22, 23.   [2] John 3 : 3, 6.   [3] John 5 : 12.

[4] There may have been wide divergence among theologians in the explanation and the philosophical placing of regeneration, but they were at one in emphasizing the fact. For outline statement see Shedd, *Dogmatic Theology*, II., 490 *sq.* And yet at this point the Ritschlian school seems weakest.

and the divine personalities — a process that is with Jesus no more figurative than the ordinary change which is wrought in the characters of two friends through their constant intercourse. It is precisely at this point that the unique significance of Jesus as an ethical teacher appears. So far from divorcing morals and religion, or from making morals the basis of religion, he makes religious experience the fountain head of good conduct, and in his own life gave a concrete illustration of his philosophy. He revealed God and he revealed also the possibilities of human life. It is not necessary to follow the straitest sect of the orthodox to appreciate the truth of this revelation made by Jesus of divine sonship. Nor is it necessary to follow the mystic into the heights of his ecstasy.[1] The thought of Jesus himself is very simple and concrete. By sonship he meant an actual likeness in the characters of men and God. And this likeness while made possible by the original capacities of humanity is something more distinct. It is the result of the influence of God upon a man's

[1] And one is tempted to add, the newer Ritschlian school into the mysteries of a new birth that can be neither " seen nor grasped, but only believed in," something which it is " absurd to suppose can be experienced as a process in time." See Hermann, *The Communion of the Christian with God.*

heart.   Those who thus have come under the renewing influence of the Divine Spirit are none the less themselves.   On the contrary, they have found themselves[1] in their new ideal — the perfection of their Father.[2]   And, if we may so use the other form this saying takes, the expression of this new family character is to be expected in deeds of kindness and mercy.[3]   Sometimes Jesus, full of the Divine Spirit, represents himself as furnishing the new life with moral impulses as the vine furnishes life to its branches.[4]   Sometimes his followers are conceived of as plants which his Father had planted.[5]   Yet always the new phase in life is the soil out of which noble impulses are to grow.   The doing of noble deeds,[6] the keeping of the commands of Jesus,[7] these are the tests of the new and divine living that comes from the impact and the infusion of divine life. From the heart thus changed will be the issues of a new life.   As Paul expresses it, the fruits of the spirit are love, joy, peace, longsuffering, kindness, goodness, faithfulness, meekness, self-control.[8]   So that, although the new man is not

[1] Matt. 10 : 39. Compare Luke 15.
[2] Matt. 5 : 48.
[3] Luke 6 : 36.
[4] John 15 : 1.
[5] Matt. 15 : 13.
[6] John 15 : 4.
[7] John 14 : 15; 15 : 10.
[8] Gal. 5 : 22.

a perfect man, he will progress towards perfection, for he is a new sort of man, a prodigal faced towards home.[1]

IV

And here, as the outgrowth of this central thought of his system, we find a second element in Jesus' philosophy of social progress; *the love that springs from a sense of brotherhood.* Two men, brothers in the physical sense, love each other instinctively, spontaneously. So in the case of this new fraternity, of this genetic relationship that exists between two men and God. If each is a son of God, are they not brothers?[2] If once they realize their common nature, will they not love one another? So at any rate thought Jesus. Love between a man and his enemy was a thing to be commanded,[3] but not between brothers.

[1] Harris, *Moral Evolution*, p. 243.

[2] While this would hold true in a sense, in case it be applied to the universal fatherhood of God and brotherhood of man, as Jesus uses the terms they gain greatly in force. As a matter of fact, does a recognition of the universal brotherhood of men prompt to special deeds of kindness in any such way as a realization of some wretch's earnest effort to grow nobler and more Godlike? On the other hand it should be noted that the term " brother " is not coextensive with " church member " any more than the kingdom of God is coextensive with the church. To narrow Jesus to such definitions would be contrary to the entire spirit of his teaching.

[3] Matt. 5 : 44.

That was to be expected.[1] Anything that pre-
vented such fraternal feeling was to be removed,
even at the cost of religious punctuality.[2] It is
true that if men fail to appreciate their fraternal
relations when they exist, they will need the command to love one another.[3] But this, like all law,
is but a provisional matter. As the realization of
their relations to one another as members of a
fraternity deepens, men will love less and less from
a sense of duty and increasingly from impulse.
And this new love was to be like Jesus' own,
ready for any sacrifice that might seem necessary.[4]

But evidently at this point we are dealing with
social motives. A man thus inspired is no longer
living for his individual, his atomistic self, but for
his social, his altruistic self. In his revelation of
the love of God and the possibility of a new and

[1] Matt. 5 : 47; 18 : 21, 22.   [2] Matt. 5 : 21-24.

[3] John 13 : 34; 15 : 12. Yet even here the example of Jesus
himself is to be an incentive.

[4] But self-sacrifice is not the central principle of Christianity as
some urge. A man must be ready to sacrifice himself if there be
need, but sacrifice in itself may be wrong. The centre of the teachings of Jesus cannot be found in any such ascetic notion of life. It
lies in the person of Jesus himself — that object-lesson in the divine
life in human life. Love involves self-sacrifice, but self-sacrifice does
not of necessity involve love.

Nor does self-sacrifice mean self-annihilation, be it from never so
holy motives. Jesus is the last man to preach either Nirvana or
pantheism.

divine sonship, Jesus prepared the way not only
for the saving of each individual sinner. He did
more. Every man who comes thus into a conscious reinstatement in the love of God, becomes
also a brother of all other men in the same relation. And so is set in motion a multitude of fraternal loves which, disregarding place, and time,
and birth, and social station, will forever remain
unsatisfied until they express themselves in recip-
rocal deeds of kindness and bring in a new social
order, in which each man will seek to minister,
not to be ministered unto; to become a servant of
all.[1]

V

If now we look somewhat more closely at
this new social force which is the dynamic side
of the apprehension of brotherhood (which it
must not be forgotten is itself the outcome of
the new and divine life in man), it will be evident that it is in itself composed of something
more than mere emotional elements, and that
Jesus regarded it as involving to an equal extent the will.[2] Were it otherwise it would be

[1] Matt. 20: 26–28.

[2] It is not necessary for such a view to strain the difference
between ἀγαπάω and φιλέω with their cognate forms (Trench,
New Testament Synonyms). The two words were used in the later
Greek somewhat indiscriminately.

o

impossible to see how one whose love was thus the outgrowth of the sense of a new reality could ever be expected to love a person in whose case the reality was not appreciable. Such a love, it would be urged, is perhaps understandable in the case of two persons who answer Jesus' conception of brothers, but would be inconceivable between one man who was a member of the kingdom, and another man who was not. How then could there be progress, or how could the kingdom fail to become a close corporation? But if the full sweep of Jesus' teaching be considered, it will be seen that this spontaneous love that arises from the sense of kinship may be directed towards one's enemies. It may, perhaps, not always be possible for one to feel the affection for one's opponents that seems to have been felt by Jesus,[1] but one can always treat one's enemies *as if* they were brothers. In such a case the conduct inspired by loving affection outlines the way for duty. The same kindness that was done spontaneously for a lover is now to be done from the sense of obligation for a persecutor.

And what will these acts be? Jesus does not specifically bid the member of the kingdom to

[1] Matt. 23: 37.

do much else than pray for and bless those who
are planning his harm; [1] but after all his meaning is not hard to find.   Both the spontaneous
love and the controlled love will seek the accomplishment of those conditions which go to
make up Jesus' ideal society.   Circumstances
will naturally determine different means and
different processes, but the love that springs
from a sense of brotherhood, will never be satisfied until it has established a social order in
which fraternity will characterize all phases of
social life.   Sometimes such impulse and duty
will need instruction, and this, it has appeared,
Jesus has given in broad principles; but in special cases, he seemed to believe that the divine
life within man thus enlightened could be
trusted to work out better and more Christian
social institutions. [2]

Therefore it has been that those times and
places in which men have come most under the
influence of the words and life of Jesus have
been those in which institutions at variance with
fraternity — branding, polygamy, the exposure of
children, slavery, drunkenness, and licentiousness
— have disappeared.   Indeed, one might almost
say, that there has been no healthy progress

<hr>

[1] Matt. 5 : 44.   [2] John 16 : 13.

towards fraternity except as it has sprung from the sense of this divine kinship. Pleas and battles for justice have wrought revolutions and wrecked institutions; but only when they have been supplemented and corrected by this fraternal impulse have they yielded the peaceable fruits of righteousness.

VI

Thus Jesus is thoroughly consistent with himself. The new social order which he outlines is not beyond the powers of man as he conceives them. It is true that a moral regeneration of the individual is presupposed before society as such can be perfected, but here Jesus is true to human capacities. Religion, just as much as selfish calculation, is one of the motive forces in human life, and to disregard it is to throw away the most powerful source of moral impulse. Therefore it is that while one may perhaps wonder that Jesus should have counted to so small a degree upon other forces that have made forward movements successful, it is quite impossible to say that he has erred in thus centring attention upon the religious side of man's nature and upon that enthusiasm for humanity which is the outgrowth of a perception of the consequent new human fraternity. Life is indeed something more than search for creature comforts. Those men of the past who have marked stages in the march of the race have always so judged. Take from the goodly company of the men who have permanently benefited society, those men whose impulses have not in some way sprung from the sense of God or the sense of fraternity, and how many will be left? In his revelation of divine sonship and the consequent human brotherhood, Jesus has furnished the basis for lasting social progress. For if humanity is to become a family inspired by the love of the divine Father, there is no power in earth or hell that can prevent the realization of the noblest social ideals of which the world has dreamed.

CHAPTER IX

THE PROCESS OF SOCIAL REGENERATION

THIS, then, is the core of the social doctrine of
Jesus — divine sonship and consequent human
brotherliness. This it is that gives unity to his
varied teachings, and, with all the moral force
it involves, is that upon which he believed could
be based the development of his kingdom. Nay,
may we not say, the moral force generated by
the revelation of this new divine and human
relationship could be trusted itself to work out
reforms? If this were the position of Jesus, it
would in large measure explain how it came
about that, except as already indicated, he gave
so few detailed directions as to specific reforms.
Was he indifferent to the process of regeneration? Or did he in the case of both individual
and society anticipate if not the details, at least
the general character, of those struggles and de-
velopments that have resulted from the work-
ings of Christianity? To put the question in

another form.   Has Christianity in its attempts
to regenerate humanity followed the directions
of Jesus or of some other man?

I

It is by no means impossible that one should
have agreed with the presentation thus far made
of the teaching of Jesus and yet hesitate to believe that the future of the kingdom as he conceived of it involved either universality or even
appreciable progress.   It is not uncommon to
commit Jesus to the belief that the new kingdom was to be hardly more than an extended
Israel into which a few Gentiles might be admitted.[1]   That an unknown, uninfluential Jew
like Jesus should have had visions of a universal
empire does, it must be granted, seem somewhat
remarkable.   Yet no one can read the words that
he spoke during the latter part of his career[2]
without being convinced that in his expectations

[1] Wendt, *Teaching of Jesus*, II., 350–351.   See also the commentary on Acts (10:1; 15:1) in the Meyer series.

[2] Thus John 12:30: I, if I be lifted up from the earth, will
draw all men unto me.   Luke 13:29: They shall come from the
east and the west and shall sit down in the kingdom of God.   *Cf.*
John 17:18, 20.   It cannot escape notice that Wendt's position
depends largely upon his belief that Jesus expected that the kingdom would be completely established during the lifetime of his
own generation.   *Teaching of Jesus*, II., 345.

the process of regeneration was not one to be limited by either geographical or political boundaries. Nor, even if it be granted as altogether probable that he did not foresee the astonishing changes wrought within Christendom, does a complete synthesis of his words permit the view that this ignorance extended to the general nature of the process that was to lead to the end of one age and the full establishment of that new social order in which God and righteousness and love were to be supreme. If it be objected that Jesus declared that few found the strait gate and the narrow path,[1] it will be enough to reply that such a remark applied to the immediate circle of his hearers and must be correlated with the other sayings in which he anticipates the evangelization and conquest of the world. Similarly, in ascribing due weight to those sayings of his in which he spoke of his contemporaries seeing the fulfilment of his prophecies of the coming kingdom,[2] one must remember that this coming was a progression whose inauguration in the new opportunities arising from the fall of the Jewish state might come suddenly, but whose completion was lost in the depths of omniscience itself.[3] In fact, if we are to regard

[1] Matt. 7 : 13, 14.   [2] Matt. 24 : 34.   [3] Matt. 24 : 36.

the "great commission"[1] as representing in any faintest way a thought of Jesus, the conclusion cannot be avoided that he was concerned with the evangelization of the world quite as much as with that of Judea and Galilee. The fact that he himself seems deliberately to have declined such wider labors[2] is to be explained as a part of a well-ordered plan in which his own evangelistic work consisted fundamentally in the gathering of a few devoted followers who should be so imbued with his own spirit as to become at once the instructors and the nucleus of a new society. The audacity of Jesus in assuming that a group of such men had within it the possibility of indefinite expansion is equalled only by the superb optimism that saw possibilities of infinite good in humanity. In both lay his philosophy of the growth of the new social order. If his teaching had been less human and humanity less capable of moral rebirth, he would have been but one of the motley crew of Christs who have so often appeared only to delude and destroy.

[1] Matt. 28: 19.

[2] John 12: 20–32. The well-known correspondence between Abgarus, king of Edessa, and Jesus, though undoubtedly apocryphal, expresses correctly, perhaps through some tradition, the attitude of Jesus: "I must fulfil all the ends of my mission in this country."

II

There is disappointment in store for the man
who looks to Jesus for specific teachings as to
reform.   He was singularly unconcerned with
those specific injunctions with which the system
of Moses teems.   There was no lack of vices
within the Roman Empire, not yet feeling the
weakly revivifying touch of poverty and philosophy, against which he might have thundered,
to say nothing of those larger questions that
might be expected to engage the attention of a
developing society.   Yet with none of these did
he concern himself.   The gospel was to be no
new collection of moral precepts to be forced
upon a world already surfeited with good advice,
but a power that should make towards righteousness.   The process of the new birth of the Jewish and heathen world was not to be that of a
new subjection to law, be it never so inspired,
but that of a growth that showed itself through
such institutions as the process of evolution
might show necessary.   The symbol of the new
society was not to be that of stones, graven
though they might be by the hand of God, but
the seed which, planted in the field, grows, one
knows not how, and in proper season produces

the blade, and the ear, and the full corn in the ear.[1]

Thus the general nature of this progress is described by Jesus as an evolution, although it could not be expected that he would use the word.

It is to be the transformation of existing powers. This does not, however, commit Jesus to the belief that all that is necessary for the attainment of a perfect ideal of social life is simply the development of a godless sociability. As has already appeared, Jesus looked upon the religious capacity of men as just as truly normal and human as any other of the capacities of human life. Accordingly, when he trusted to humanity to develop into something like normal living, it was because he had recognized the religious forces resident in human nature which were capable themselves of great development and which possessed the power of transforming character. The world, or the existing social environment in which the new society found itself, was to be won over to the Christian conceptions of social relations by virtue of the fact that it contained within it material which might be regenerated through an apprehended God. Jesus was no Christ for animals, but for men. Because the world was evil did not

[1] Mark 4: 26–28.

argue that it was unsavable. If the leaven was
to leaven the lump, it must have been because the
lump was leavenable. Out from the seething
mass of men and women so largely under the
control of evil purposes and unbrotherly ideals,[1]
there was to be formed a body whose ideals were
to be noble and fraternal. They were to be the
same individuals, but transformed; no longer the
enemies one of another, but brothers, each look-
ing not alone to his own affairs, but also in the
spirit of helpfulness to the affairs of another.

This process is by analogy organic. The kingdom does not depend upon accretion for its
growth, but upon the assimilation of new material won from the environment in which it may
find itself. It is indeed surprising to see how
frequently Jesus recurs to biological analogies in
describing the future progress of his kingdom.
One can hardly with safety revert at this point to
the important figure of the leaven, since its biological content could hardly have been explicitly in
the mind of Jesus. But within the sphere of

[1] "The foreigner is a wolf" was altogether a more characteristic
social conception of the ancient world than the noble words of an
Epictetus. One has but to read the *Golden Ass* of Apuleius to see
how, in the midst of a well-developed commercial system, there
lingered a conception of travellers hardly higher than that held by
brigands.

observable organic growth Jesus saw in the life
of plants repeated analogies of the growth of that
which he did but inaugurate.   Now the progress
of the kingdom is like that of the mustard seed; [1]
now of the seed sown on soils which by their different natures condition the size of the harvest; [2]
again it is like the seed that must grow if once it
be planted, since the earth itself compels it — a
most instructive analogy. [3]   From a somewhat
different point of view, the history of the kingdom
in the world seemed to be like that of a field in
which tares and grain grew side by side until the
harvest; [4] and, most beautiful and suggestive of
all, the efficiency of the members of the new
family was distinctly taught to depend upon the
closeness of their union with himself, as branch
with vine. [5]   Such a habit of thought can hardly
be said to have been fortuitous.   It is too nearly
akin to the conception of the new kingdom as a
family to permit the interpretation that Jesus did
not intend to emphasize the truth that back of
any permanent social growth there must be, first
of all, a sympathy in purpose and similarity in
capacity, such as can be compared alone to the
apprehension and the assimilation of parts of its

[1] Matt. 13:31.   [3] Mark 4:27.   [4] Matt. 13:24–30.
[2] Mark 4:3 *sq.*   [5] John 15:4 *sq.*

environment by the living organism. Indeed, when once Jesus' conception of "the world" is clearly gained, the analogy becomes altogether striking. The kingdom of a few men, filled with the might that comes from the experience of a newly revealed sonship of God and brotherhood with each other, is seen set down in the midst of societies full of opposite forces, yet composed of convertible men. Out from this social environment the little group is to select and convert and assimilate whom it can and what institutions it can. Through these newly acquired elements it will grow, ever more capable of further growth, like the seed in the ground nourished and made great by the surroundings within which it finds itself.

But at one point the analogy fails. Jesus never for an instant thought of the kingdom as ultimately merely a world within a world. The plant can never make the earth from which it grows wholly its own and itself, but there was to be no such dualism in the case of society. With the modification to be considered presently, Jesus expected the new society to be at last coextensive with all society; or more truly, he expected that at last the world would be so thoroughly transformed into the kingdom as to cease to be distinct from it.   The three measures of meal would all be leavened.   The prince of this world had already been judged,[1] the twelve were to sit as judges of the new Israel,[2] the Son of Man was at last to come in the glory of an undisputed ruler.[3]

But evidently this process of assimilation must be preceded by a transformation that is moral.[4] Evil men are not to share in the joys of this new society.   It is not enough with Jesus to improve the conditions of human life.   The mere conquest of matter, the exploitation of natural resources, as seen clearly enough to-day, need not of necessity imply any essential advance in civilization.   To clothe a man and to feed him well, to enable him to build up great buildings and establish large businesses, to enable an entire people so to develop its land and its mineral deposits as to become rich, may be the furthest possible from building that person or that people into a more fraternal life.   To each alike comes the warning of Jesus: "Thou fool, this night thy soul shall be demanded of thee."[5]   But to bring the constructive forces of a man or a nation into subjection to lofty ideals; to make that which is

[1] John 16:11.
[2] Matt. 19:28.
[3] Matt. 16:27; 19:28; 25:31.
[4] Matt. 12:33; 7:17, 18; 12:34, 35.
[5] Luke 12:20.

wrong hated and that which is good loved; so to transform and improve and ennoble a man that instead of seeking his own selfish interests he will find his life by spontaneously losing it in the society of other lives about him; to develop a love for men because one is one's self a child of God; in a word, to make normal social life depend upon goodness — that is the fundamental position of Jesus. One does not need to be reminded that in this he stands by no means in the same class with many other would-be reformers. To give large wages, to make the home more comfortable and happy, to see that the sanitary arrangements of the city and community are perfect, to provide a fair income, healthful food, good amusements, and all the other requirements of respectable life to-day; to do this and let evolution do the rest — this is the position of more than one social teacher.

But the imperfection that must needs be corrected, in the estimation of Jesus, was no chance of birth or occupation in life. The Pharisee was quite as ill as the harlot and the publican.[1] The cause of all inequality and lack of fraternity is moral; it is sin. Men cannot reach that divine sonship in which fraternal love becomes natural

[1] Matt. 21 : 31.

so long as the spirit of selfishness rules them. A corrupt tree cannot bring forth good fruit.[1] The world can become the kingdom only by a repentance and a moral change on the part of its members that replaces the spirit of revolt against goodness and a loving God with the spirit of sonship.[2]

And Jesus saw aright. A perfect society cannot be created from imperfect people. That which stands in the way of the realization of many a man's ideal for society has not been its own logical inconsistency, but its failure to find or to produce the right sort of men upon which to work. The plan of the house called for marble and the only material at hand was mud. Jesus proposes to furnish good material as well as a noble plan.

Such a moral transformation of humanity's sinful but potentially noble nature must of necessity be gradual. It cannot be accomplished in a generation. An impatient man with a passion for hastening his benefactions would have failed to see this necessity. At the outset of his public life Jesus had wrestled with the temptation to hurry the conquest of the world,[3] but as he stood at the end of his ministry and saw the

[1] Matt. 7 : 17.   [2] John 3 : 3.   [3] Matt. 4 : 8–10; Luke 4 : 5–8.

P

months of earnest effort that lay behind him, and judged of the future, the progress of his kingdom appeared not as a thing to be accomplished by social cataclysms,[1] but rather as the steady growth of a tiny seed into a great tree.[2]

It is in the course of this gradual development of a fraternity that attempts to assimilate an unregenerate society that we must especially look to find Jesus' conception of the process by which his kingdom was to reach its completion.

III

Is this process to be institutional and national, or is it to be individualistic ? Is society or are men first to be regenerate ? It is a thought that finds frequent expression that Christianity introduced individualism. So indeed did Christianity, if by individualism is not meant an atomism. For the Christian doctrine of society is not that of an aggregation of individuals made repellent through uncompromising demands for rights. The only sense in which Christianity can claim to be individualistic is in its elevation of the worth of each human life. But the real worth of every life

---

[1] John 18 : 30.   [2] Cf. Matt. 13 : 31-33.

consists not in separate existence, but rather in the identification of its interests with the interests of others in the exercise of that fraternal love which was both the ideal and the practice of Jesus himself.

Yet a society must be composed of individuals, and therefore it was that Jesus devoted himself so largely to the individual. Reformations do not proceed *en masse*. There must be the successive winning of one man after another until there be developed something like a nucleus of a more perfect social life. The method, therefore, of Jesus in the founding of the kingdom was not the wholesale righting of political or economic or religious wrongs, although when this was necessary he did not hesitate to give vent to his righteous indignation against men who persisted in perpetuating them.

Rather was his method the successive winning of separate souls, now a Philip and now a Peter, until at last he had discovered and won to himself a few men and women who were so far imbued with his own spirit of fraternity as to be ready to inaugurate and evangel a higher and more perfect social life. Loyola never followed more persistently or more successfully a Xavier, John, a fugitive robber, than did Jesus the humble fishermen with whom his lot was cast. Once let the spirit of such brotherliness become regnant, and all the horrid brood of vices that spring from its opposite will vanish. Men may need to incorporate this spirit in special laws, but this must be done by each age and community for itself. Jesus gives a constitution; men can frame statutes.

At one point, however, he may be said to have given specific directions for social life. The member of the kingdom will submit to abuse rather than become involved in strife. He will turn his left cheek to him who strikes his right; he will let cloak follow coat rather than go to law; he will go two miles with him who would force him to go one.[1] Could rules be simpler?

Simple indeed these rules appear, but few of Jesus' teachings are more difficult to estimate. Shall we with Tolstoi regard their literal readings as the very core and centre of Christian doctrine, or shall we with easy indifference thrust them back into the depths of the mystery of oriental hyperbole? Are they to be blindly followed, or are they to be skipped?

The proper point of view from which to get their perspective is given by Jesus' insistence upon reconciliation as an expression of fraternal love.

[1] Matt. 5 : 39–41.

He who has done a brother an injury is to obtain forgiveness before he attempts to worship God at the altar.[1] But not only this, he who has suffered an injury must not wait for such an advance, but must himself come to an agreement with his persecutor if it be in any way possible. In a word, reconciliation must not wait upon repentance.[2] This seemed as difficult to the disciples as to later ages. They thought there must at least be some limit to forgiveness — that seven times would exhaust human nature.[3] But the answer of Jesus showed that in his estimation any surrender of pride was better than the perpetuation of a cause of dissension.[4] And if the offender after orderly admonition and appeal prove incorrigible, it is better to break with him utterly than to run the risk of increased bitterness and strife.[5] If a house and a kingdom divided against themselves could not stand, much less a family.

It is in the light of this imperative demand for unity in a fraternity and for the opportunity for an unimpeded exercise of brotherliness that these other and more extreme words of Jesus must be regarded. They are no new or central teaching,

[1] Matt. 5: 22–24.   [3] Matt. 18: 21.   [4] Matt. 18: 22–35.
[2] Matt. 18: 15.   [5] Matt. 18: 15–17.

but a new phase of the great teaching of fraternity as it extends itself to those who have not yet come under its influence. As between the members of the Christian society there must be brotherly unity, so between them and those who are not fellow-members there is to be at the cost of any sacrifice maintained a bond of peace that shall make possible the transformation of an unloving and evil world. Old laws of retaliation are here absolutely iniquitous.[1] No persecution or oppression or insult, be it never so stinging, is to give grounds for a refusal to let love beget reconciliation. Jesus knew the strength of the desires for revenge and justice, and he knew also how impossible would be the conquest of the world by men who were constantly stickling for their rights, or who in a spirit of revenge attempted to bring their enemies to justice. It was a severe teaching, but from his point of view inevitable. It were better to suffer wrong than to attempt to win the world to love by fighting with it. Forgiveness should be spontaneous, and, if need be, he who had been injured must be the one to make advances toward a reconciliation.

And did Jesus thereby let down the bars for a mad incursion of evil doers? Would he have men

[1] Matt. 5 : 38, 39.

never protect themselves from injury or punish criminals? Would he have swindlers and thieves and every sort of rascal prey upon a society that should never seek to purge itself of its criminal classes? The questions would answer themselves even if we did not have the caution of Jesus not to throw pearls before swine,[1] and the example of his caution in fleeing from danger,[2] and his denunciations of hypocrites and embezzlers.[3] Goodness in Jesus was not divorced from common sense, and non-resistance in the sense of a willingness to forego contention and even a just punishing of one's personal enemies, is not the same as the attempt a society should make to reform some of its members by righteous punishment. There was to be a burning of the tares quite as certainly as a gathering of the sheaves into barns.[4] But in a sense, the individual has little to do with such corporate — or, as Jesus would rather say, divine — judgments. His duty is simple: by unselfish love so to win over his neighbors to his own higher ideals and to the imitation of Christ that the need of even reformatory punitive action may grow less, and all men may come increasingly into that life in which social service grows ever more

[1] Matt. 7 : 6.
[2] John 7 : 1.
[3] Matt. 23 : 27, 28; Luke 20 : 45-47.
[4] Matt. 13 : 30.

spontaneous because of the new motives that are furnished by the new consciousness of brother-hood.

And yet it can be objected, and with truth, that, as the term is commonly used, good men will not of necessity make a good society. It is possible to develop virtue in such a fashion as to make its possessors unattractive, and, if not self-centred, at least incapable of aggressive work for the help-ing of surrounding lives. If this were the legiti-mate result of Christian teaching, one could well despair of a Christian society. But it is sufficient answer to the objection to point to the life of Jesus. In him we see a perfect incarnation of his teach-ings, and no man can study his life without feeling that a society composed of Christs would be a perfect fraternity. No man feels the same in regard to Socrates. A thousand men of his ilk would constitute a very uncomfortable community within which to live. The same is true of societies composed of ascetic or semi-ascetic reformers. But so normal was Jesus' life, so judiciously de-voted to the welfare of others, so regardful of the conventionalities which experience begets as regu-lators of social life, that he stands as a representa-tive of an individual who has found his completest mission in the identification of his life with that of

other men.   Indeed, precisely in the same proportion that a man imitates the life of Jesus as an
individual does he help establish Jesus' fraternal
society.

IV

The expanding Christian society, therefore, will
consist of groups of men and women each possessed of the same spirit and method of life as that
taught by their Master.   These little groups of
individuals Jesus likened to leaven which was
thrown into the meal and there remained until it
had leavened the meal.   Though they are not of
the world, yet they are to stay in it.[1]   Conquest,
not flight, is to be their watchword.   The progress
of Christian society in the world will depend upon
the power which each nucleus of Christian persons gathered into a society will have upon the
surrounding social life.   It can expand only by
transforming and assimilating to itself this environment.   As the process is not one of mere instruction but of the impartation of new life, Jesus must
have had in mind certain means by which this
impartation could be accomplished.   And these
means we should expect would be such as would
render especially easy the bringing of individuals
under the influence of those forces which would

[1] John 17: 15.

make them fraternal by making them Christlike. Does Jesus specify or imply any such?

In the larger sphere of life Jesus seems indirectly to recognize the power of public opinion in modifying environment. There is, it must be granted, a certain Christianization of society going on unconsciously. The life of genuine members of the kingdom has an influence upon those who are outside its professed members that is as real as it is unmeasurable. For do they not contribute something to the formative ideals and opinions of their society? Through the influence of individuals who have come under the influence of Jesus, others are constantly forced to adopt higher standards in at least conventional morality. Yet the force of public opinion, so far as Jesus recognizes it, appears at first glance largely evil. His apostles were not to be of the leaven of the Pharisee; [1] they were not to pattern themselves after the habits of the hypocrite; [2] they were not, to use the Pauline expression, to "conform to the present world." [3] But it is not difficult to see that such a vitiated public opinion must be replaced by a new and better as soon as hypocrites are replaced by honest men. If one is not to

---

[1] Matt. 16:11; Mark 8:15; Luke 12:1.
[2] Matt. 6:2, 5, 16.   [3] Rom. 12:2.

conform to a bad social standard it is certainly
incumbent upon him to erect a new. Here Jesus'
influence must be most felt in working deliverance
for the poor of to-day's society. He cannot be
expected to be ever working miracles for the benefit of the needy. His regenerating power must lie
in the new consciences and sympathies of those
who are following his teachings and who attempt
to express his principles in legislation and industrial life. The optimistic Psalmist could see divine
care for the poor where to-day's pessimism sees
only greed and iron laws. A public opinion that
shall express the real fraternity that Jesus aimed
to establish would show that divine care is not inconsistent with economic principles, and that the
true expression of the Father's love is a brother's
aid.

The earliest attempts which the primitive Christians made towards the incorporation of the
kingdom of God were, like those of their Master,
in the line of philanthropic effort. Peter and John
healed the lame man in lieu of alms,[1] and within
the little body of believers themselves one of the
first expressions of the new social spirit was in the
sharing of wealth among the brethren.[2] In charity
there has always been a point of contact between

[1] Acts 3 : 1 *sq.*   [2] Acts 2 : 44.

the Christian society and the world that has been of the greatest service. Charity is of necessity not a permanent need of the world, if ever the kingdom of God is to be realized, but as social life is constituted to-day Jesus saw that it was of the very utmost importance. He worked out the details of the social obligations of men of wealth with deliberation and firm touch. In giving dinners they are to treat poor people as their equals, even though they cannot expect equivalent return for social favors.[1] The buyer of land and oxen, as well as the new-made husband, are seen by Jesus to serve as the type of those who, because of their own indifference, are to be replaced at the king's supper by those of the highways and hedges.[2] And if wealth is to be devoted to social purposes it must be with no sense of superiority or unaccompanied by the giver's sympathy and love. The poor widow, he said, gave more than the rich, though she gave but two mites,[3] and the neighborliness of the good Samaritan was certainly seen less in his expenditure of money than in his services to the unfortunate traveller.[4] As Paul later so finely said, if one were to give all his goods to feed the poor, and had not love, it would profit him

---

[1] Luke 14:13.

[2] Matt. 22:1-10; Luke 14:16-24.

[3] Mark 12:41-44.

[4] Luke 10:30 sq.

nothing.[1]   One's own desires are to be the measure of acts that affect others.[2]   Accordingly, the frequent reference to almsgiving[3] can have little other meaning than that it may serve as a means of furthering the reign of fraternity.   It is not an end in itself; like all other good deeds it must cause its beholders to glorify the Father in heaven.[4]   Through it the attention and good will of men might be gathered, one foundation of the new social order, brotherly love, made more manifest, and thus many brought to a union with older believers whose fellowship was with the Father and with his Son Jesus Christ.[5]

But probably the most effective and historically about the only appreciable force that has been at work in the regeneration of society has been the church.   According to one's conception of this body will one regard it as coextensive with or less in extent than the kingdom itself.[6]   If one, however, takes thought only of Jesus, it becomes reasonably clear that he was little concerned with founding a religious institution.   In the one of the two instances in which he speaks of the

---

[1] 1 Cor. 13: 3.   [2] Matt. 7: 12.

[3] Matt. 5: 42; 6: 2-4; Luke 12: 33.

[4] Matt. 5: 16; cf. Luke 19: 8.   [5] 1 John 1: 3.

[6] In the former sense we understand the word to be used by Freemantle, *The World as the Subject of Redemption.*

church[1] it is evident that it is a means to the maintenance of brotherliness; and in the other instance, the formula, "binding and loosing," that is, the right to teach authoritatively, was entrusted not to the church, but to that member of the kingdom upon whom the church was to be built.[2] Indeed, it almost seems as if in the mind of Jesus the church was simply the religious phase of the life of the kingdom. As the kingdom was to be fundamentally social the state is simply the new fraternity in its political aspect. In the same way the church expresses the combination of the members of the fraternity for the purpose of special philanthropic and religious effort. So indifferent was Jesus to the church as an institution that he never spoke of its organization, and left practically no directions for anything like a ceremonial. He founded not a church but a kingdom. Nevertheless, as society stands to-day, there can be little doubt that the chief points of contact between those who are endeavoring to incorporate the teachings of Jesus in their lives and those who are not so endeavor-

[1] Matt. 18:17.
[2] Matt. 16:18. It is by no means impossible that this text, as well as Matt. 18:17, was not contained in the earlier Logia. See Wendt, *Die Lehre Jesu*, I., 155 *sq.*

ing, are the organizations known as the churches. In the same proportion as each church develops in its appreciation of Jesus and in its endeavor to emphasize the social necessities of a perfect individual life, will its influence be felt in transforming the environment in which it is placed.

Further, it is clear that the progress of the Christian transformation of society must proceed, precisely as in the method of Jesus, along the line of conversion or, more exactly, the regeneration of the individual. At this point he who seeks to inaugurate a greater Christian society has the invaluable aid of the church's effort. For generations churches of all shades of evangelical faith have been endeavoring to lay deep this foundation of a progressive social regeneration. It has often happened that such a programme has seemed ineffectual; men have often endeavored to substitute a system of ethics for the dynamics of a personal faith in God. But such efforts have generally resulted from or preceded a weakening of conventional morals and a degeneracy in society as a whole. The test of a Christian society's *morale* has seldom been the utterances of its ethical teachers as much as the religious fervor of its masses. Strip from the England of the seventeenth century the burning zeal of the Separatist and Puritan, and we have the Restoration and the Court Preachers. Concerts and kindergartens are very necessary as complements of revivals and mission halls, but as saviours of a nation's civilization and purity they are as grass before the storm. No thoughtful man will under-estimate or antagonize the remarkable combina-tion of professional and amateur philanthropy that has within a few years burst forth in social settlements and institutional churches. But, so far as one can at present judge, such forms of social effort, profoundly Christian as they are, can never remove the need for the older and more permanent work of the missionary. No civilization can be Christian that balks at the fact of divine sonship. No social reform will be thorough-going and lasting that stops before en-deavoring to bring every human being into the righteousness and fraternal love that spring from religious experience. Evangelizing effort on the part of the church, therefore, is to be urged not merely on the ground of the benefit brought to the individual who is turned from evil to righteous-ness, but on the ground of its profound signifi-cance and helpfulness in all matters of social advance. It cannot be too often emphasized that social regeneration according to the conception of Christ cannot proceed on any other line than that of the replacing of bad men by good men. And this above all others is the function of the church. For the Christian ideal is not that of the monk but of the Christ. To aid in the regeneration of a man is to aid in the regeneration of society.

V

It is evident that such transformation of an imperfect world into the perfect family Jesus anticipated must, if this process is to be followed, require much time. So Jesus foresaw. To those people who expected that the kingdom of God would come immediately he spoke the parable of the nobleman who went into a far country.[1] Indeed, the entire completion of the transforming process was not to be reached until the end of the age — an event of such indefinite date that in regard to it he professed himself to be in ignorance. And not only was it to be slow, but it was to be full of struggle and anguish for those men who attempted to better humanity and human society. Jesus would, indeed, have been wonderfully lacking in foresight if his own experience had not taught him that his followers must expect bitter opposition. The master had been

[1] Luke 19 : 11 sq.

Q

called Beelzebub and had been persecuted, and
should the disciples expect to be above their
lord in escaping like treatment? It was enough
for the disciple to be like his master.[1] Helpful
as the new doctrine might be, Jesus saw that it
was such as might well be judged revolutionary
by those whom its insistence upon equality and
fraternity might alienate. His was not a mission
wholly of peace.[2] He came to bring both sword
and fire into social life.[3] The members of the
new propaganda were to expect severe treatment
at the hand of Roman and Jew alike. They
were to go forth as sheep among wolves.[4] Political power and ecclesiasticism would equally set
themselves against them.[5] But there was to be
no compromise. He who would be saved must
endure to the end.[6] That which they heard in
the ear they were to tell on the housetop.[7] They
were to be cities on hills, lamps uncovered by
bushels, salt that had not lost its savor.[8] There
was nothing hidden except that it should be revealed.[9] And at the same time no members of the
kingdom were to yield to revengeful feelings and

[1] Matt. 10: 24, 25.
[2] Matt. 10: 34.
[3] Luke 12: 49.
[4] Matt. 10: 16.
[5] Matt. 10: 17; 23: 34; Luke 12: 11; 21: 12.
[6] Matt. 10: 22.
[7] Matt. 10: 26 *sq.*; Mark 4: 21 *sq.*
[8] Matt. 5: 13–15.
[9] Mark 4: 22; Luke 8: 17.

lead revolution.   On the contrary their arms were to be prayer and benediction.[1] As the forces upon which he had counted for success were peaceful, so as far as his followers were concerned, was to be the process by which the unwilling world would be transformed into the kingdom.[2]

Yet a startling thing in this calm anticipation of a slow and painful process is his recognition of the possibility of a time when the forces of human nature should be insufficient; when the new social order would be so far established as to have transformed and assimilated all of the transformable material it found in its environment.   Until that time, of necessity the two opposing worlds must have existed side by side.[3] Like tares and wheat growing in the same field men were to grow together until good and bad alike had exhausted the possibilities of growth. Then, through some exercise of the supreme power of the heavenly Father and King, the

[1] Luke 6: 38.

[2] One should not overlook, however, the balance in Jesus' mind throughout all this dark forecast of the future. He cautions his followers against quixotic adventures. They were not to cast their pearls before swine (Matt. 7: 6). Because of the dangers to which they were to be exposed, while as harmless as doves, they were to be as wise as serpents (Matt. 10: 16).

[3] Matt. 13: 24-30.

agony and the transformation were to cease together. As tares are separated from the wheat, those incorrigible men who refused to share in the new sonship and fraternity would be removed, and thereafter the righteous were to shine like the sun in the kingdom of their Father.[1]

As to when this supplementing of growth by cataclysm shall come, Jesus gives us no information. But that he should have seen the necessity of it is a tribute to his sense of reality. Men of persistent anti-filial and anti-fraternal disposition can never be made into loving brethren. Their removal is the only hope of a permanently peaceful fraternity. Just what Jesus meant by the striking imagery in which he clothed this thought we cannot clearly see. That it may mean revolution or some other tremendous political change is not clear and yet not to be absolutely denied in the light of his references to the destruction of Jerusalem. But, whatever it may be, it will mark the triumph of the new social order. Penal action will reach its consummation in the isolation of offenders. Individual and institutional life will no longer testify to the reign of even an enlightened selfishness. The world will, by virtue of man's

[1] Matt. 13:43.

endeavor and God's regenerating power, have been transformed into the kingdom. And the triumph of this new and perfected humanity, this eternal fraternity which he described and instituted and for which centuries have travailed — this is the coming of the Lord.

"There remaineth, therefore, a Sabbath rest for the people of God." So wrote the author of the epistle to the Hebrews as he looked back upon a restless, defeated theocracy, and forward towards the future of the true Judaism.[1] So, too, many a man beaten back in his endeavor to bring to an unwilling world Christ's blessing of brotherliness and love has looked towards the East, hoping that through the darkness of the sin and misery and social inequality of the world in which he lived there might break the dawn of that great Sabbath. And although we may no longer expect a new Jerusalem with streets of gold and walls of jasper, we too wait for a city in which God shall be King and Father and in which love shall lead to justice and righteousness to joy. For it is no dream or apocalypse that meets us in the words and life of Jesus, but rather a teaching the embodi-

[1] Heb. 4:9.

ment of which is well worth an effort. He who to-day feels humanity's need and appreciates the crisis in which the world is gripped, will not rashly push one side the ideals and powers that he revealed who, by his life and words, has already rewrought civilizations as has no man or teaching.

INDEX OF TEXTS

SOCIAL EVOLUTION.

BY

BENJAMIN KIDD.

New Edition, revised, with a New Preface.

Cloth. 8vo. $1.75.

EXTRACTS FROM SOME OF THE PRESS NOTICES.

" The name of Mr. Benjamin Kidd, author of a very striking work on
' Social Evolution,' is, so far as we know, new to the literary world; but it
is not often that a new and unknown writer makes his first appearance
with a work so novel in conception, so fertile in suggestion, and on the
whole so powerful in exposition as ' Social Evolution ' appears to us to be,
. . . a book which no serious thinker should neglect, and no reader can
study without recognizing it as the work of a singularly penetrating and
original mind." — *The Times* (London).

" It is a study of the whole development of humanity in a new light, and
it is sustained and strong and fresh throughout. . . . It is a profound work
which invites the attention of our ablest minds, and which will reward those
who give it their careful and best thought. It marks out new lines of study,
and is written in that calm and resolute tone which secures the confidence
of the reader. It is undoubtedly the ablest book on social development
that has been published for a long time." — *Boston Herald.*

" Those who wish to follow the Bishop of Durham's advice to his clergy
—' to think over the questions of socialism, to discuss them with one another reverently and patiently, but not to improvise hasty judgments ' — will
find a most admirable introduction in Mr. Kidd's book on ' Social Evolution.'
It is this because it not merely contains a comprehensive view of the very
wide field of human progress, but is packed with suggestive thoughts for
interpreting it aright. . . . We hope that the same clear and well-balanced
judgment that has given us this helpful essay will not stay here, but give us
further guidance as to the principles which ought to govern right thinking
on this the question of the day. We heartily commend this really valuable
study to every student of the perplexing problems of socialism." — *The
Churchman.*

THE MACMILLAN COMPANY,

66 FIFTH AVENUE, NEW YORK.